History Summarized

WORLD WAR II

EUROPEAN AND NORTH AFRICAN FRONTS

WORLD
BOOK

www.worldbook.com

World Book, Inc.
180 North LaSalle Street
Suite 900
Chicago, Illinois 60601
USA

For information about other "History Summarized" titles, as well as other World Book print and digital publications, please go to **www.worldbook.com**.

For information about other World Book publications, call 1-800-WORLDBK (967-5325).

For information about sales to schools and libraries, call 1-800-975-3250 (United States) or 1-800-837-5365 (Canada).

Library of Congress Cataloging-in-Publication Data for this volume has been applied for.

History Summarized
ISBN: 978-0-7166-3800-1 (set, hc),

World War II—European and North African Fronts
978-0-7166-3810-0 (hc.)

Also available as:
ISBN: 978-0-7166-3820-9 (e-book)

Printed in China by Shenzhen Wing King Tong Paper Products Co., Ltd., Shenzhen, Guangdong
1st printing July 2018

STAFF

Writer: Tom Firme

Executive Committee

President
Jim O'Rourke

Vice President and
Editor in Chief
Paul A. Kobasa

Vice President, Finance
Donald D. Keller

Vice President, Marketing
Jean Lin

Vice President, International
Maksim Rutenberg

Vice President, Technology
Jason Dole

Director, Human Resources
Bev Ecker

Editorial

Director, New Print
Tom Evans

Manager
Jeff De La Rosa

Editor
Mellonee Carrigan

Librarian
S. Thomas Richardson

Manager, Contracts and
Compliance
(Rights and Permissions)
Loranne K. Shields

Manager, Indexing Services
David Pofelski

Digital

Director, Digital Product
Development
Erika Meller

Digital Product Manager
Jonathan Wills

Manufacturing/Production

Manufacturing Manager
Anne Fritzinger

Production Specialist
Curley Hunter

Proofreader
Nathalie Strassheim

Graphics and Design

Senior Art Director
Tom Evans

Coordinator, Design
Development and Production
Brenda Tropinski

Senior Visual
Communications Designer
Melanie Bender

Senior Designer
Isaiah Sheppard

Media Editor
Rosalia Bledsoe

Senior Cartographer
John M. Rejba

TABLE OF CONTENTS

"History Summarized"

   Each book in this series concisely surveys a major historical event or interrelated series of events or a major cultural, economic, political or social movement. Especially important and interesting aspects of the subject of each book are highlighted in feature sections. Use a "History Summarized" book as an introduction to its subject in preparation for deeper study or as a review of the subject to reinforce what has been studied about the topic.

What were the European and North African fronts of World War II?

World War II (1939-1945) was the most destructive war in history. It killed more people, destroyed more property, and disrupted more lives than any other war in history. It probably had more far-reaching consequences than any other war. The war brought about the downfall of Western Europe as the center of world power. It led to the dominance of the Soviet Union and the United States, and set off a power struggle between the two countries called the Cold War. World War II also opened the nuclear age.

It is impossible to say exactly how many people died in World War II. Estimates suggest that about 20 million soldiers died during the war's six years. From 30 million to 40 million civilians also perished. That makes a combined death toll of 50 million to 60 million people.

The battlegrounds of World War II spread to nearly every part of the world. Troops battled in the deserts of North Africa. They fought on the islands and seas of the Pacific Ocean. Battles raged on the frozen steppes (vast plains) of the Soviet Union and in the cities, forests, and farmers' fields of Europe. Submarines fought below the surface of the Atlantic Ocean.

World War II began on Sept. 1, 1939, when Nazi Germany invaded Poland. Germany's powerful war machine rapidly crushed Poland, Denmark, Luxembourg, the Netherlands, Belgium, Norway, and France. In June 1940, Fascist (*FASH ihst*) Italy joined the war on Germany's side. In western Europe, only the United Kingdom remained. The United Kingdom resisted German air attacks that destroyed great sections of

5

German soldiers swept into Poland in armored and motorized divisions on Sept. 1, 1939. The invasion was the beginning of World War II. Germany's powerful war machine rapidly crushed Poland, Denmark, Luxembourg, the Netherlands, Belgium, Norway, and France.

London and other cities. German and Italian forces then clashed with the British in Greece and northern Africa. In June 1941, Germany invaded the Soviet Union, breaking its nonaggression pact of 1939. In that treaty, the two nations had promised not to attack each other.

Bulgaria, Hungary, Romania, and the German-created states of Croatia and Slovakia eventually joined the Axis. In opposition, the United Kingdom, the United States, the Soviet Union, and China formed the core of the Allies. The Allies totaled 50 nations by the end of the war.

During 1942, the Allies stopped the Axis advance in northern Africa,

the Soviet Union, and the Pacific. Allied forces landed in Italy in 1943. They reached France in 1944. In 1945, the Allies drove into Germany from the east and the west. Germany surrendered on May 7, 1945. Japan surrendered on Sept. 2, 1945.

An uneasy peace took effect as a war-weary world began to rebuild after World War II. Much of Europe lay in ruins. Tens of millions of people were dead. Millions more were starving and homeless. The United States and the Soviet Union emerged as the world's most powerful nations. But new threats to peace arose.

At the end of World War I (1914-1918), representatives of the victorious nations met at the Paris Peace Conference in France in 1919 to dictate the peace. The Treaty of Versailles punished Germany severely. Germany vowed to ignore the treaty and avenge its defeat.

CHAPTER ONE

Causes of World War II

In 1919, after the end of World War I (1914-1918), representatives of the victorious nations met in Paris, France, to dictate the peace. The treaties of the Paris Peace Conference followed more than four years of costly and bitter warfare. The treaties were worked out in haste by countries with opposing goals. The agreements failed to satisfy even the victors. Of the countries on the winning side, Italy and Japan left the peace conference most dissatisfied. Italy gained less territory than it felt it deserved. It vowed to take action on its own. Japan gained control of German territories in the Pacific and launched a program of expansion. Yet Japan felt slighted by the peacemakers' refusal to endorse the principle of the equality of all races.

The defeated countries in World War I—Germany, Austria-Hungary, Bulgaria, and the Ottoman Empire—were especially dissatisfied with the Peace of Paris. (The Ottoman Empire comprised what today is the nation of Turkey and parts of northern Africa, southwestern Asia, and southeastern Europe.) They were stripped of territory and arms. They were also required to make *reparations* (payments for war damages).

The Treaty of Versailles (*vehr SY*) punished Germany severely. Its representatives signed the treaty only at the threat of invasion. Many Germans resented the "war guilt clause" that forced Germany to accept sole responsibility for causing World War I.

World War I damaged European countries' economies. Both the winners and the losers came out of the war in debt. The defeated powers had difficulty paying reparations to the victors. The victors had difficulty repaying loans from the United States. The global economic shift from war to peace left millions of veterans unemployed. Millions of others who had worked in munitions factories and other war-related industries lost their jobs.

Italy and Japan suffered from overcrowding and a lack of resources after World War I. They eventually tried to solve their problems by territorial expansion. In Germany, *hyperinflation* (rapid, uncontrolled price increases) made money worthless. People lost their life savings. In 1924, loans from the United States helped stabilize Germany's currency. The reparation payment schedule was relaxed. By the late 1920's, the economic situation in Germany—and the rest of Europe—had improved.

Then came the Great Depression, a worldwide economic downturn. It began in the United States in 1929. By the early 1930's, the global economic crisis had halted and reversed Europe's economic recovery. The Great Depression caused mass unemployment, spreading poverty and despair. It weakened democratic governments while strengthening extreme political movements that promised to end the economic crisis.

Two movements in particular gained strength. The forces of Communism, known as the left, called for revolution by the workers. The forces of fascism, called the right, favored strong national government. Throughout Europe and elsewhere, the forces of the left gained ground against the forces of the right. Political extremes gained support in countries with the greatest economic problems and the deepest resentments of the Peace of Paris.

Nationalism was an extreme form of patriotism that swept across Europe beginning in the 1800's. Supporters of nationalism placed loyalty to their nation above any other public loyalty. They defined nationality

Nazi rallies in Germany featured thousands of troops and deeply impressed the German people. German dictator Adolf Hitler (1889-1945) used the rallies to persuade the nation to accept his plan of conquest for Germany, which was humiliated by its defeat in World War I and the harsh terms of the peace treaty. Hitler turned Germany into a powerful war machine and provoked World War II.

by language and ethnicity. They viewed foreigners and minority groups with suspicion and scorn. Such beliefs helped nations justify their conquests of other lands. Such ideas also helped justify the poor treatment of minorities within their borders. Nationalism was a chief cause of World War I. It grew even stronger afterward.

Nationalism corresponded with feelings of discontent. The more people felt deprived of national honor, the more they wished to see their country powerful and able to insist on its rights. Many Germans felt humiliated by their defeat in World War I and the harsh terms of the Treaty of Versailles. During the 1930's, they enthusiastically supported the National Socialist German Workers' Party—the Nazis (*NAHT seez*). The Nazi Party glorified Germany's position in the world and vowed to make the nation strong again.

The League of Nations was an international organization
created to maintain peace following World War I. The League
ceased to function with the outbreak of World War II. This
image shows the official opening of the League on Jan. 10, 1920.

The Peace of Paris established an international organization called the
League of Nations to maintain peace. But nationalism and individual
arguments prevented the League from working effectively. Each country
backed its own interests at the expense of those of other countries. Only
weak countries agreed to submit their disagreements to the League of
Nations for settlement. Strong nations reserved the right to settle their
disputes by threats or even force.

During the 1920's and 1930's, political unrest and poor economic
conditions enabled radical dictatorships to come to power in the Soviet
Union, Italy, Germany, and Japan. The dictators held total power and
ruled without regard to law. They used terror and secret police to crush

opposition to their rule. People who objected risked imprisonment or execution.

Communists, led by V. I. Lenin (1870-1924), seized power in Russia in 1917. The Soviet Union was established in 1922. A dictatorship set up by Lenin controlled the country by the time he died in 1924. After Lenin's death, Joseph Stalin (1879-1953) and other leading Communists struggled for power. Stalin eliminated his rivals one by one, taking total control in 1929.

In Italy, economic distress after World War I led to strikes and riots. Out of the violence, a strongly nationalistic group called the Fascist Party gained many supporters. Benito Mussolini (*beh NEE toh moos soh LEE nee*) (1883-1945), leader of the Fascists, promised to bring order and prosperity to Italy. Mussolini vowed to restore to Italy the glory the country had known in the days of the ancient Roman Empire. By 1922, the Fascists had become powerful enough to force the king of Italy to appoint Mussolini as prime minister. Mussolini took the title *Il Duce* (*eel DOO chay*), which means "The Leader." He began to establish an *authoritarian* state—that is, one that valued obedience to authority above individual freedom.

In Germany, the Nazi Party made huge gains during the Great Depression. In 1933, Adolf Hitler (1889-1945), the leader of the Nazis, was appointed chancellor of Germany. Hitler, who was called *der Führer* (*dair foo ruhr*), meaning "the Leader," rapidly increased his own power. He vowed to ignore the Versailles Treaty and avenge Germany's defeat in World War I. Hitler preached that Germans were a "superior race." He called Jews and Slavs inferior. He began a campaign of hatred against Jews and Communists and promised to rid the country of them. In this time of distress and depression, Hitler's extreme nationalism appealed to many Germans.

Adolf Hitler and World War II

Adolf Hitler (1889-1945) ruled Germany as dictator from 1933 to 1945. He turned Germany into a powerful war machine and provoked World War II in 1939. Hitler's forces conquered most of Europe before they were defeated in 1945.

Hitler spread death as no person has done in modern history. "Have no pity! Act brutally!" he told his soldiers. He ordered tens of thousands of those who opposed him to be executed and hundreds of thousands to be thrown into prison.

Hitler particularly persecuted Jews. He ordered them killed in countries he controlled. Hitler set up concentration camps where about 4 million Jews were murdered. Altogether, Hitler's forces killed about 6 million European Jews as well as about 5 million other people that Hitler regarded as racially inferior or politically dangerous.

Adolf Hitler began his rise to political power in 1919, the year after World War I had ended. The German Empire had been defeated, and the nation's economy lay in ruins. Hitler joined a small group of men who became known as *Nazis*. He soon became their leader. Hitler and his followers believed he could win back Germany's past glory. He promised to rebuild Germany into a mighty reich (*ryk*), or empire, that would last a thousand years.

Many people did not take Hitler seriously. But his fiery words and brilliant blue eyes seemed to hypnotize those who listened to him. Many Germans believed he was their protector and friend. His emotional speeches made crowds cheer "Heil, Hitler!" ("Hail, Hitler!").

Hitler became dictator of Germany in 1933 and quickly succeeded in regaining some territories taken from Germany as a result of World War I. He threatened war against Czechoslovakia in 1938 but was stopped by a combination of counter-threats and concessions. His forces invaded

In 1939, German dictator Adolf Hitler appeared before the Reichstag, the elective legislative assembly of Germany (now called the Bundestag), to address the Jewish Question. During his brutal rule, Hitler persecuted Jews, which he regarded as racially inferior. He ordered the killing of about 6 million European Jews as well as about 5 million other people.

Poland in 1939. Then, the United Kingdom, France, Australia, New Zealand, South Africa, and Canada declared war on Germany, and World War II began.

Hitler had a clear vision of what he wanted, and he had the daring to pursue it. But his aims had no limits, and he overestimated the resources and abilities of Germany. Hitler had little regard for experts in any field. He regularly ignored the advice of his generals and followed his own judgment, even while Germany was being defeated in the last years of the war. From 1933 onward, Hitler prepared Germany for war. He rearmed the nation, first secretly, then in open violation of the Treaty of Versailles. No nation acted to stop him, and so Hitler's steps became bolder. Hitler planned to establish Germany as the world's leading

In March 1938, German troops marched into Austria without opposition and annexed the country as part of Nazi Germany. Many people in both countries welcomed the union of Austria and Germany.

power and to destroy the Jewish people.

Soon after Hitler took power in Germany, he began to build up Germany's armed forces. The build-up violated the Treaty of Versailles. In 1936, Hitler sent troops into the Rhineland. The Rhineland was an area in western Germany that the treaty had made a *demilitarized zone,* a neutral zone free from military control. His generals had opposed this dangerous challenge to France. But Hitler guessed correctly that France would not stop him. The stationing of German troops in the Rhineland was the first of the Nazi dictator's victories without war.

In March 1938, Hitler's troops invaded Austria. Austria then became part of Germany. Many people in both countries welcomed the *Anschluss* (*AHN shlus*) (union) of Austria and Germany.

In September, France and Britain consented to Hitler's occupation of the German-speaking areas of what then was Czechoslovakia, which previously had been part of the empire of Austria-Hungary before World War I ended. After this move, Hitler said he wanted no more territory. But after each success, he planned a new takeover. He took control of the rest of Czechoslovakia in March 1939.

Poland came next on Hitler's list. But Britain and France tried to stop any further German expansion. They guaranteed Poland's independence, saying that they would go to war against Germany if Hitler attacked Poland. Hitler doubted that they would do so. In August 1939, Germany and the Soviet Union signed treaties of friendship. On September 1, 1939, Germany invaded Poland. Britain and France declared war on Germany two days later.

Adolf Hitler (front row, fourth from right) watches his Nazi troops advance into Poland in September 1939. Hitler is joined by Nazi police commander Heinrich Himmler (on Hitler's left).

Hitler's armies overran Poland in just a few weeks. In the spring of 1940, they easily conquered Denmark, Norway, the Netherlands, Belgium, Luxembourg, and France. On June 22, 1940, France signed an armistice with Germany.

Britain fought on alone. A major German air offensive failed to weaken British resistance. Hitler kept delaying an invasion of Britain. Instead, he considered invading the Soviet Union. He explained to his generals that Britain would not surrender until its last potential ally on the European continent had been defeated.

In June 1941, the attack on the Soviet Union began. At first, the German forces made rapid progress. But their advance began to slow in November. By December, it was halted outside Moscow. An unusually bitter winter, Soviet reinforcements, and supplies sent by the United States helped the Soviet forces stop the Germans and begin to push them back during the winter. Renewed German attacks in 1942 and 1943 could not break through. During the Battle of Stalingrad, which lasted for five months during 1942 and 1943, the Soviets wiped out an entire German army of 300,000 men. This German defeat was a major turning point in the war.

While his empire lasted, Hitler directed the storm troopers, Nazi officials, and members of the army and the civil service in a campaign of mass slaughter. About 6 million Jews—over two-thirds of the Jews of Europe—were murdered. More than 3 million Soviet prisoners of war were starved and worked to death. Hitler's victims also included large numbers of Poles, Slavs, Roma (sometimes called Gypsies), Jehovah's Witnesses, priests and ministers, mental patients, homosexuals, Communists, and other political opponents.

The German resistance had tried since 1938 to kill Hitler and overthrow the Nazis. But repeated plots failed. On July 20, 1944, Hitler

Members of the Nazi Party marched in a rally in Nuremberg, Germany, in 1933. Their banners bore the Nazi emblem, the swastika. The Nazi Party gained control of Germany in 1933.

narrowly escaped death when a German Army officer placed a bomb in Hitler's briefing room.

Early in 1945, the Allies marched into the heart of Germany against rapidly dwindling opposition.

By April 1945, Hitler had become a broken man. His head, hands, and feet trembled, and he was tortured by stomach cramps. Eva Braun, Hitler's mistress since the 1930's, joined him at his headquarters in a bomb shelter under the Reich Chancellery in Berlin. She and Hitler were married there on April 29. The next day, they killed themselves. Aides burned their bodies. Seven days later, Germany surrendered.

In 1935, Italian troops invaded Ethiopia, one of the few independent countries in Africa at the time. The Italian forces were led by General Achille Starace (on the left, on horseback).

German aggression and appeasement

In 1935, Italian troops invaded Ethiopia. At that time, Ethiopia was one of the few independent countries in Africa. The Italians used machine guns, tanks, and airplanes to overpower Ethiopia's poorly equipped army. In 1939, Italy swept through Albania, in southeastern Europe. Albania was another easy conquest for Mussolini.

In 1936, Germany and Italy agreed to support each other's foreign policy. The alliance was known as the Rome-Berlin Axis (*AK sihs*). Japan joined the Axis in 1940. It then became the Rome-Berlin-Tokyo Axis.

A civil war tore Spain apart from 1936 to 1939. In 1936, many of Spain's army officers revolted against the government. The army rebels chose General Francisco Franco (1892-1975) as their leader. Franco's forces were known as Nationalists or Rebels. The forces that supported Spain's elected government were called Loyalists or Republicans. The Spanish Civil War drew worldwide attention.

Hitler and Mussolini sent troops, weapons, aircraft, and advisers to aid the Nationalists. The Soviet Union was the only power to officially help the Loyalists. France, the United Kingdom, and the United States did not intervene. But Loyalist sympathizers from many countries joined the International Brigades to fight in Spain.

Spain's dictator, General Francisco Franco (seated in vehicle), arrives in San Sebastian after winning the Spanish Civil War in April 1939. World War II broke out five month later.

The last Loyalist forces surrendered on April 1, 1939. Franco set up an authoritarian government in Spain. The Spanish Civil War served as a military proving ground for weapons and tactics that were later used during World War II. The conflict in Spain foreshadowed the coming war. It pitted forces of the radical right—Nazis and Fascists—against the rest of the world.

Czechoslovakia had become an independent nation after World War I. Its western region of Bohemia (*boh HEE mee uh*) was surrounded on three sides by Germany. Hitler sought control of the Sudetenland (*soo DAYT uhn land*), the German-speaking border areas of Bohemia. More

Two European dictators, Adolf Hitler of Germany (left) and Benito Mussolini of Italy (right), dreamed of powerful empires. Their actions plunged much of Europe and Africa into World War II.

Huge crowds of people gathered in Wenceslas Square in Prague, Czechoslovakia, to celebrate after the country declared its independence from the Austro-Hungarian Empire on Oct. 28, 1918. Germany invaded Czechoslovakia (now the Czech Republic and Slovakia) in 1939 and occupied the country for most of World War II.

than 3 million people of German descent lived there. Urged on by Hitler and his agents, Sudeten Germans clamored for union with Germany.

Czechoslovakia refused to concede territory. Hitler prepared to strike. France and the Soviet Union pledged to support the young nation against German aggression. As tension mounted, the United Kingdom wished to preserve peace at all cost. Prime Minister Neville Chamberlain (*CHAYM buhr lihn*) (1869-1940) believed war could be prevented by meeting Hitler's demands. That policy became known as *appeasement*.

Chamberlain had several meetings with Hitler during September 1938 as Europe edged closer to war. Hitler raised his demands at each meeting. On September 29, Chamberlain and French Premier Édouard Daladier (*ay DWAHR dah lah DYAY*) (1884-1970) met with Hitler and Mussolini in Munich (*MYOO nihk*), Germany. Chamberlain and Daladier agreed to turn over the Sudetenland to Germany, forcing Czechoslovakia to accept the agreement. Hitler promised to demand no more territory in Czechoslovakia.

The Munich Agreement marked the height of the policy of appeasement. Chamberlain and Daladier hoped that the agreement would satisfy Hitler. They hoped it would prevent war—or at least prolong the peace until the United Kingdom and France were ready for war. The two leaders were mistaken on both counts.

Prime Minister Neville Chamberlain (1869-1940) of the United Kingdom waves the Munich Agreement upon his return to England in 1938. The agreement was an attempt by the United Kingdom and France to prevent war by meeting some of Germany's demands.

Germany broke the Munich Agreement when its army entered Prague, Czechoslovakia, in March 1939 and seized the Czech provinces of Bohemia and Moravia. German troops are shown here marching through the gates of Prague Castle.

The failure of appeasement soon became clear. Hitler broke the Munich Agreement in March 1939 and seized the rest of Czechoslovakia. He thereby added Czechoslovakia's armed forces and industries to Germany's military might. In the months before World War II began, Germany's preparations for war proceeded faster than did the military build-up of the United Kingdom and France.

Germany's seizure of Czechoslovakia symbolized Hitler's hunger for domination, which Chamberlain and Daladier underestimated. Britain, France, and the rest of Europe stood unprepared for how aggressively Germany would attack countries across the continent. Germany would strike quickly, and the Allied forces took time to effectively counter its attacks.

Munich Agreement

The Munich Agreement, made on Sept. 29, 1938, in Munich, Germany, was an attempt by the United Kingdom and France to prevent war by agreeing to German demands for more territory. The two nations granted Germany's demand for the Sudetenland, a German-speaking region in what was then Czechoslovakia, believing Germany would, in return, end its aggressive expansion. But Germany soon violated the agreement by seizing more of Czechoslovakia, tilting Europe toward World War II.

At the end of World War I (1914-1918), the Sudetenland became part of the new country of Czechoslovakia. The region had about 2,800,000 Germans and about 800,000 Czechs. It covered about 11,000 square miles (28,500 square kilometers). Czechoslovakia had military outposts throughout the mountainous Sudetenland to defend against German invasion.

Germany annexed Austria in March 1938. Hitler then threatened to invade Czechoslovakia. He claimed that the Czechoslovak government was mistreating German residents of the Sudetenland. That summer, Germany began preparing to invade.

British Prime Minister Neville Chamberlain sought a way to avoid war. He twice met with Hitler in September, but their negotiations failed. On September 28, Hitler invited Chamberlain, as well as leaders Edouard Daladier of France and Benito Mussolini of Italy, to a conference. It took place in Munich on September 29 and resulted in the Munich Agreement.

The pact allowed Germany to annex the Sudetenland. It called for a commission to supervise Germany's occupation of the region and to define the new border. The United Kingdom and

British Prime Minister Neville Chamberlain (from left), the French leader Edouard Daladier, German dictator Adolf Hitler, and Italy's Benito Mussolini met in Munich, Germany, in 1948.

France also agreed to protect Czechoslovakia from aggression. But Germany and Italy said they would guarantee Czechoslovakia's borders only after Polish and Hungarian claims to areas they had lost to Czechoslovakia were settled. The Munich Agreement at first seemed to have prevented war. Chamberlain returned to cheering crowds in England and announced "peace in our time."

In March 1939, Hitler violated the agreement and sent German troops to invade western Czechoslovakia. Germany attacked Poland on September 1. On September 3, the United Kingdom and France declared war on Germany, and World War II began.

The German occupation of Czechoslovakia brought widespread suffering to the country. At the end of World War II, the Sudetenland again became part of Czechoslovakia. The Czech government then expelled over 2 million Germans from the region.

The Munich Agreement became the classic example of a failed policy of *appeasement*—that is, making concessions to an aggressive nation to avoid war. After Munich, such agreements were thought to invite war rather than to prevent it.

Poland had a large army, but little modern equipment, during World War II. Polish troops (shown here) fought bravely when Germany invaded Poland on Sept. 1, 1939, but they were no match against the speed and surprise of the German blitzkrieg.

CHAPTER TWO

Early stages of the war

During the first year of World War II, Germany won a series of swift victories. It conquered the nations of Poland, Denmark, Luxembourg, the Netherlands, Belgium, Norway, and France. Germany then attempted to bomb the United Kingdom into surrendering, but failed.

The port city of Danzig (*DAN sihg*), which today is Gdańsk (*guh DAHNSK*), and the province of East Prussia were separated from Germany by the Treaty of Versailles. In March 1939, Hitler demanded the city's return, as well as access to East Prussia. Poland refused. The United Kingdom and France pledged to help Poland if Germany attacked it. Yet the two powers could aid Poland only by invading Germany. Neither wanted to take that step. The United Kingdom had only a small army. France had prepared to defend its territory, not to attack.

The United Kingdom and France hoped that the Soviet Union would help defend Poland. But Germany's Hitler and the Soviet Union's Stalin shocked the world by becoming allies. On Aug. 23, 1939, Germany and the Soviet Union signed a nonaggression pact. In the agreement, they promised not to go to war against each other. They secretly planned to divide Poland between themselves.

On Sept. 1, 1939, Germany invaded Poland, beginning World War II. Poland had a large army, but little modern equipment. Polish leaders expected to fight along the country's frontiers. However, the Germans introduced a new method of warfare called *blitzkrieg* (*BLIHTS kreeg*), or lightning war. The blitzkrieg stressed speed and surprise. Rows of tanks smashed through Poland's defenses and rolled deep into the country before the Polish army had time to react. Swarms of German dive bombers and fighter aircraft knocked out communications and pounded battle lines. More than 1 million German troops swept across the Polish plains.

The Poles fought bravely, but the German attack threw the Polish army into confusion. Adding to Poland's troubles, Soviet forces invaded from the east on Sept. 17, 1939. Within two weeks, the Soviet Red Army occupied the eastern third of Poland. Germany had swallowed up the rest. When the fighting stopped on October 6, over 60,000 Polish troops were dead. So were tens of thousands of civilians. The Germans lost more than 10,000 killed in action.

The United Kingdom and France declared war on Germany on Sept. 3, 1939, two days after the invasion of Poland. But the two countries did little while Poland collapsed. France moved troops to the Maginot (*MAZH uh noh*) Line. The line was a belt of steel and concrete fortresses it had built along its border with Germany. The United Kingdom sent a small force into northern France. Germany stationed troops on the Siegfried (*SEEG freed*)Line, a strip of defenses Hitler built in the 1930's opposite the Maginot Line. The two sides avoided fighting in late 1939 and early 1940. Journalists called the period the "Phony War."

After the outbreak of war in September 1939, Denmark, Finland, Norway, and Sweden announced their neutrality. Germany depended heavily on Swedish iron ore shipments through neutral Norway. Hitler feared British plans to cut off those shipments by laying explosives in Norway's coastal waters. On April 9, 1940, German forces invaded Norway and Denmark. Denmark surrendered the same day. The United Kingdom tried to help Norway. But Germany's air power prevented

British troops march over a bridge into a French underground fortress covered with vegetation at the Maginot Line, a fortified line of defense in eastern France along the French border with Germany.

many British ships and troops from reaching the country. Norway surrendered on June 10, 1940. The conquest of Norway secured Germany's shipments of iron ore. It also provided bases for German submarines and aircraft. About 5,000 Germans were killed in the conquest. So were more than 6,000 Allied troops (British, French, Norwegian, and Polish).

Chamberlain, who had favored appeasement, resigned after the invasion of Norway. Winston Churchill replaced him as the United Kingdom's prime minister on May 10, 1940.

The Low Countries—Belgium, Luxembourg, and the Netherlands—hoped to remain neutral after World War II began. However, Germany launched a blitzkrieg against them on May 10, 1940. Luxembourg surrendered in one day. The Netherlands gave up in five days. British and French forces rushed into Belgium and fell into a German trap. As the Allied forces raced northward, the main German invasion cut behind them through the Belgian Ardennes (*ahr DEHN*) Forest to the south. The Germans reached the English Channel on May 21. They had nearly surrounded the Allied forces in Belgium.

King Leopold III of Belgium surrendered on May 28, 1940. The surrender left the Allied forces in Belgium trapped. They retreated to the French seaport of Dunkerque (*DUHN kuhrk*) on the English Channel. To rescue the troops, the United Kingdom sent all available seacraft. The fleet of "little ships" included destroyers, yachts, ferries, fishing vessels, and motorboats. Under heavy enemy fire, the hastily assembled fleet safely ferried about 338,000 troops to England from May 26 to June 4.

The relief of Dunkerque saved many soldiers to fight another day. About 35,000 Allied troops were left behind. So were tens of thousands of vehicles and tanks. The British Royal Air Force (RAF) lost more than 100 warplanes protecting the evacuation.

France had expected to fight along a stationary battlefront. The country had built the Maginot Line to defend the front. But in May 1940, German tanks and aircraft passed around the line. They swept through Luxembourg and Belgium and into northern France. On June 5, the Germans launched a major assault along the Somme River. The Somme had been the scene of brutal slaughter in World War I. The blitzkrieg overwhelmed the French forces, driving them mercilessly backward. Seeing an opportunity to profit from Germany's success, Italy declared

On June 22, 1940, French and Nazi military leaders met in a railroad car at Compiegne, France, for the formal surrender of France during World War II. German General Wilhelm Keitel (standing, left) reads the agreement.

war on France and the United Kingdom on June 10. The French government fled from Paris to Bordeaux (*bawr DOH*) the same day.

German troops entered Paris on June 14, 1940. French Premier Paul Reynaud (*reh NOH*) wanted to fight on. But many of his generals and cabinet officers believed that the battle for France was lost. Reynaud resigned. A new French government agreed to an *armistice* (truce) on June 22.

Dunkerque

The Battle of Dunkerque (*DUHN kuhrk*) (also spelled Dunkirk or Dunquerque) was fought between German and Allied troops during World War II. It took place in May 1940 at the French port of Dunkerque. The battle was a major victory for the Germans over the Allies. However, Dunkerque became famous for the dramatic rescue of hundreds of thousands of Allied soldiers. The Battle of Dunkerque was part of the larger Battle of France, which ended with France's surrender to Germany on June 22, 1940.

In May 1940, Germany invaded Belgium. The invasion forced the defending Belgian, British, and French troops to retreat to Dunkerque, across Belgium's border with France. German warplanes and tanks soon attacked Dunkerque's defenses. On May 24, the Germans halted their tank advance toward Dunkerque. The halt, which lasted for two days, gave the Allies time to organize an evacuation of their threatened troops.

To rescue the troops, the United Kingdom sent all available seacraft. The fleet of "little ships" included destroyers, ferries, fishing vessels, motorboats, and yachts. Under renewed German assault, the boats carried soldiers from the beach at Dunkerque to larger warships offshore. The soldiers then were brought to England.

From May 26 to June 4, the rescue effort ferried about 338,000 Allied troops safely from Dunkerque to England. About 35,000 soldiers were left behind, along with tens of thousands of vehicles and tanks. The British Royal Air Force lost more than 100 warplanes protecting the evacuation. The

The evacuation of Dunkerque rescued about 338,000 Allied soldiers in 1940. While the Germans attacked, troops were ferried to safety aboard every available British vessel, including this destroyer preparing to dock at Dover, England.

Germans sank 6 British destroyers and more than 200 smaller ships. Another 220,000 Allied troops were eventually rescued from French ports.

The Battle of Dunkerque was a crushing defeat for the Allies. However, the rescue effort enabled the Allies to fight another day. The British expression "Dunkerque spirit" describes the ability to rally in the face of adversity.

Under the terms of the armistice, Germany occupied the northern two-thirds of France and a strip of western France along the Atlantic Ocean. Southern France remained in French control. The town of Vichy (*VIHSH ee* or *vee SHEE*) became the capital of unoccupied France. Marshal Henri Philippe Pétain (*ahn REE fee LEEP pay TAN*) (1856-1951), a French hero of World War I, headed the Vichy government. He largely cooperated with the Germans. Then in November 1942, German troops occupied all of France.

One of the French generals, Charles de Gaulle (*duh GOHL*) (1890-1970), escaped to the United Kingdom after France fell. In radio broadcasts to France, he urged the people to carry on the fight against Germany. The troops who rallied around de Gaulle became known as the Free French.

During the conquest of the Netherlands, Belgium, Luxembourg, and France, about 27,000 German troops died. More than 100,000 Allied soldiers lost their lives. The dead included about 90,000 French.

The Royal Air Force (RAF) Fighter Command of the United Kingdom lost nearly half its strength in the Battle of France. The Germans took some time to coordinate newly captured air bases and prepare to attack yet again. The British took advantage of this precious time to replace the planes and pilots lost over France. Flyers from Australia, Canada, Czechoslovakia, New Zealand, Poland, South Africa, and elsewhere helped replenish the ranks. Prime Minister Churchill told Parliament: "What General Weygand called the Battle of France is over. The Battle of Britain is about to begin." (General Maxime Weygand commanded the French Army during the German invasion of France during World War II.)

Hitler believed that the United Kingdom would now seek peace. The British, however, were determined to resist the Nazis. The United Kingdom fought on alone. Hitler prepared to invade southern England in a

German forces entered Paris, France, on June 14, 1940. Here, German soldiers march through the Arc de Triomphe, a famous landmark in the French capital, on the broad avenue called the Champs Elysees. France agreed to an armistice days later.

military operation with the code name *Sea Lion*. But before an invasion force could safely cross the English Channel, Hitler had to clear the RAF from the sky. The Battle of Britain was the first battle ever fought solely for air supremacy.

In July 1940, the German air force, the Luftwaffe, began to attack RAF and Royal Navy bases. Germany's bombers and fighter planes outnumbered the RAF's fighters by more than 4 to 1. But the previous Luftwaffe victories had come against nations with inferior air forces. The RAF had two outstanding types of pursuit planes—the *Hurricane* and the *Spitfire*. The RAF had also greatly developed the new technology of radar. RAF radar stations could detect German squadrons as they left their airfields in France.

An area of London lies in ruins after German dictator Adolf Hitler unleashed his air force on English cities in what is known as the Blitz. German planes bombed cities from London to Manchester daily and then nightly for months. More than 40,000 British citizens lost their lives.

The air campaign was violent and costly for both sides. Of the nearly 3,000 British and Allied pilots who took part in the Battle of Britain, more than 500 were killed. The RAF lost about 900 aircraft. For the Germans, it was worse. Germany lost around 1,750 aircraft along with 2,600 aviators and crew. Operation Sea Lion was scrapped. But the bombing continued.

Hitler had originally ordered that no civilian targets should be attacked. However, in late August, a lost Luftwaffe pilot violated his orders and bombed central London. An outraged Churchill retaliated with a bombing attack on Berlin. Hitler then unleashed his air force against English cities. He thus began what is known as the *Blitz*. German planes bombed cities from London to Manchester day after day, then night after night for months. Raids continued throughout the winter and spring. Finally, in May 1941, Germany gave up its attempts to defeat the United Kingdom from the air. More than 40,000 British civilians had lost their lives.

Hitler's decision to switch attacks from RAF bases to British cities effectively won the battle for the United Kingdom. It allowed the RAF to constantly replace both planes and pilots. The United Kingdom's survival became important later in the war. The island served as an airfield and base for the Allied invasion of Europe. The British Army and High Command also made crucial contributions to the ultimate Allied victory.

Within a year after the evacuation at Dunkerque, the Allies built momentum in the war, culminating in the biggest early Allied victory in the Battle of Britain. The strategic shift by Hitler to bomb British cities was his first major overreach in World War II, which he would later make on the Soviet front and elsewhere. While Germany attacked in different directions, Italy pushed for victories of its own.

Battle of Britain

The Battle of Britain was a decisive air conflict between British and German forces during World War II. Having crushed France, Poland, and Czechoslovakia in 1939 and 1940, the Germans had only to defeat the United Kingdom to win the war in western Europe. Hermann Göring (*HEHR mahn GEHR ihng*) (1893-1946), commander of the *Luftwaffe* (German air force), argued that the Luftwaffe alone could reduce British resistance. Luftwaffe officers believed that an invasion of England would be possible once Germany had destroyed the British Royal Air Force (RAF) and cleared the English Channel of British warships.

The Battle of Britain began on July 10, 1940, when about 60 German aircraft attacked shipping in the English Channel. For the rest of July, the Luftwaffe tested RAF defenses with repeated attacks on the Dover area. In August, the Luftwaffe extended its attacks to all the air bases in southern England. On August 15, it attacked Tyneside, in northeastern England, with 140 aircraft and launched 800 aircraft against RAF bases in the south. The RAF made 974 attacks on hostile aircraft and fought at least five major air actions. Each side exaggerated the other's aircraft losses.

In September, the Luftwaffe attacked London and the airfields of the Thames Valley. An attack by 400 German aircraft started fires in the London docks, but 53 attackers were shot down by the RAF or by antiaircraft fire. On September 15, a force of 1,300 German aircraft made a two-pronged attack on the London docks and the Southampton area. The air battle spread over southern England and lasted all day. The RAF lost 27 aircraft, and the Luftwaffe 56. The German High Command realized it could not destroy the British air defenses. The British beat off a last German force of 850 aircraft at the end of September.

The great success of the British defense was largely due to the high quality of its fighter aircraft. In addition, the Luftwaffe lost more pilots than the RAF did, because German pilots who were shot down and survived were captured, while British pilots were recovered and returned to service. The British use of radar, a new technology the Germans did not have, to give early warning of the position and approach of enemy aircraft proved vital as well.

The RAF's bravery and endurance during the Battle of Britain prompted Sir Winston Churchill's famous tribute: "Never in the field of human conflict was so much owed by so many to so few."

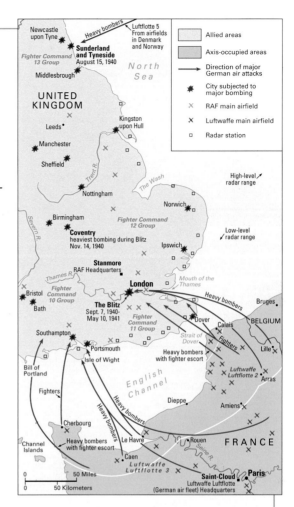

Few British cities escaped the violence of the 1940 Battle of Britain. The British Royal Air Force fought fiercely, eventually forcing the Germans to abandon the air campaign. Radar and outstanding warplanes were key to the British victory, which prevented a German invasion of the United Kingdom.

Winston Churchill and World War II

Sir Winston Leonard Spencer Churchill (1874-1965) became one of the greatest statesmen in world history. Churchill reached the height of his fame as the heroic prime minister of the United Kingdom during World War II. Churchill also was a noted speaker, author, painter, soldier, and war reporter.

Early in World War II, the United Kingdom stood alone against Nazi Germany. The British people refused to give in despite the tremendous odds against them. Churchill's personal courage, the magic of his words, and his faith in victory inspired the British to "their finest hour." The mere sight of this stocky, determined man—a cigar in his mouth and two fingers raised high in a "V for victory" salute—cheered the people.

Churchill not only made history, he also wrote it. As a historian, war reporter, and biographer, he showed a matchless command of the English language. In 1953, he won the Nobel Prize in literature. Yet as a schoolboy, he had been the worst student in his class. Churchill spoke as he wrote—clearly, vividly, majestically. Yet he had stuttered as a boy.

The vigor of Churchill's body equaled that of his mind. His tremendous physical endurance allowed him to live a long, eventful life. In youth, his boundless energy found release on the battlefield. Churchill loved the rough and ready life of a soldier, but he also had great sensitivity. He expressed this side of his nature beautifully in his paintings.

Churchill entered the service of his country in 1895 as an army lieutenant toward the end of the reign of Queen Victoria, who lived from 1819 until 1901. He ended his career in 1964 as a member of the House of Commons under Queen Elizabeth II, Queen Victoria's great-great-granddaughter.

In speaking and in writing after 1932, Churchill tried to rouse his nation and the world to the danger of Nazi Germany. The build-up of the

German armed forces alarmed him, and he pleaded for a powerful British air force. But he was called a warmonger.

German troops marched into Poland on Sept. 1, 1939. The war that Churchill had so clearly foreseen had begun. On September 3, the United Kingdom and France declared war on Germany. Prime Minister Neville Chamberlain at once named Churchill first lord of the Admiralty, the same post he had held in World War I. The British fleet was notified with a simple message: "Winston is back."

In April 1940, Germany attacked Denmark and Norway. The United Kingdom quickly sent troops to Norway, but they had to retreat because they lacked air support. In the parliamentary debate that followed, Chamberlain's government fell. On May 10, King George VI asked Churchill to form a new government. That same day, Germany invaded Belgium, Luxembourg, and the Netherlands.

At the age of 65, Churchill became prime

The mere sight of Winston Churchill, with his two fingers raised in a "V for victory" salute, cheered the British people during World War II. His courage, the magic of his words, and his faith in victory inspired the British to "their finest hour."

minister. He wrote later: "I felt as if I were walking with destiny, and that all my past life had been but a preparation for this hour and for this trial."

Rarely, if ever, had a national leader taken over in such a desperate hour. Churchill told the British people he had nothing to offer them but "blood, toil, tears, and sweat" as they struggled to keep their freedom.

The months that followed brought a full measure of blood, toil, tears, and sweat. Belgium surrendered to Germany on May 28, and the defeat of France appeared likely at any moment. On June 4, Churchill told the House of Commons that even though all of Europe might fall, "... we shall not flag or fail. We shall go on to the end ... we shall fight in the seas and oceans ... we shall fight on the beaches, we shall fight on the landing grounds, we shall fight in the fields and in the streets, we shall fight in the hills; we shall never surrender. ..." On June 22, France surrendered to Germany.

The United Kingdom now stood alone. A German invasion seemed certain. In a speech to the House of Commons on the day after France asked Germany for an armistice, Churchill declared: "Let us therefore brace ourselves to our duties, and so bear ourselves that, if the British Empire and its Commonwealth last for a thousand years, men will say, 'This was their finest hour.' "

The Germans had to defeat the Royal Air Force (RAF) before they could invade across the English Channel. In July, the German *Luftwaffe* (*LUFT vahf uh*) (air force) began to bomb British shipping and ports. In September, the Luftwaffe began nightly raids on London. The RAF, though outnumbered, fought bravely and finally defeated the Luftwaffe. Churchill expressed the nation's gratitude to its airmen: "Never in the field of human conflict was so much owed by so many to so few."

While the battle raged, Churchill turned up everywhere. He defied

General Wladyslaw Sikorski (left), head of Poland's government-in-exile, and British Prime Minister Winston Churchill inspect Polish troops in 1941.

air-raid alarms and went into the streets as the bombs fell. He toured RAF headquarters, inspected coastal defenses, and visited victims of the air raids. Everywhere he went he held up two fingers in a "V for victory" salute. To the people of all the Allied nations, this simple gesture became an inspiring symbol of faith in eventual victory.

Churchill had a strong grasp of military reality. He had denied the pleas of the French for additional support from RAF planes, knowing that the United Kingdom needed them for its own defense. He decided that the French fleet at Oran in Algeria had to be destroyed. Otherwise, French warships might be surrendered and used to strengthen the German navy. He boldly sent the only fully equipped armored division in England to Egypt. Churchill reasoned that if a German invasion of

British Prime Minister Winston Churchill (in light suit) inspects a long line of tanks and troops from a vehicle during the British victory parade in Berlin, Germany, on July 21, 1945. The troops, nicknamed the "Desert Rats," are from the British Army's 7th Armoured Division.

England could not be prevented, one armored division could not save the country. But that division could fight the Germans in Egypt.

In August 1941, Churchill and United States President Franklin D. Roosevelt met aboard ship off the coast of the Canadian province of Newfoundland (now Newfoundland and Labrador). They drew up the Atlantic Charter, which set forth the common postwar aims of the United States and the United Kingdom. Churchill and Roosevelt exchanged more than 1,700 messages and met nine times before Roosevelt's death in 1945.

The United States entered the war after Japan attacked Pearl Harbor, Hawaii, on Dec. 7, 1941. Later that month, Churchill and Roosevelt conferred in Washington, D.C. On December 26, Churchill addressed the United States Congress. He stirred all Americans with his faith "... that in the days to come the British and American peoples will ... walk together side by side in majesty, in justice, and in peace."

In August 1942, Churchill journeyed to Moscow to meet with Soviet Premier Joseph Stalin. The Soviet Union had entered the war in June 1941, after being invaded by Germany. Almost immediately, Stalin had demanded that the British open a second fighting front in western

Europe to relieve the strain on the Soviet Union. Churchill explained to Stalin that it would be disastrous to open a second front in 1942 because the Allies were unprepared.

In January 1943, Churchill and Roosevelt met in Casablanca, Morocco. They announced that the Allies would accept only *unconditional* (complete) surrender from Germany, Italy, and Japan.

The first meeting of Churchill, Stalin, and Roosevelt took place in Tehran, Iran, in November 1943. The Big Three, as they were called, set the British-American invasion of France for the following spring. In February 1945, the Big Three met in Yalta in the Soviet Union. The end of the war in Europe was in sight. The three leaders agreed on plans to occupy defeated Germany. Churchill distrusted Stalin. He feared the Soviet Union might keep the territories in eastern Europe that its troops occupied. Roosevelt, a close friend of Churchill's as well as an ally, died two months after the conference, and Harry S. Truman (1884-1972) became president of the United States.

Germany surrendered on May 7, 1945, almost five years to the day after Churchill became prime minister. In July, Churchill met with Truman and Stalin in Potsdam, Germany, to discuss the administration of Germany. But Churchill's presence at the meeting was cut short. He had lost his post as prime minister.

An election had been held in the United Kingdom. The Conservatives suffered an overwhelming defeat by the Labour party. The Labour party's promise of sweeping socialistic reforms appealed to the voters. In addition, the people were voting against the Conservative party. Many blamed the Conservatives, who had been in office before the war, for failing to prepare the United Kingdom for World War II. The defeat hurt Churchill deeply. Clement R. Attlee (1883-1967) succeeded him as prime minister.

British and Commonwealth troops march past Egypt's pyramids as part of Allied defense preparations against Italian forces. Italy invaded Egypt and other parts of Africa in 1940.

CHAPTER THREE

War spreads to Africa and the Soviet Union

By the end of 1941, World War II had become a global conflict. Battles erupted in Africa, the Balkan Peninsula of southeastern Europe, and the Soviet Union. The Axis and the Allies also battled each other at sea and in Asia. In December 1941, the United States entered the war.

The Italian army opened battlefronts in Africa in the summer of 1940. In August, Italian troops pushed eastward from Ethiopia. They overran the British forces in British Somaliland (now Somalia). The following month, forces from the Italian colony of Libya invaded Egypt.

Fighting seesawed back and forth across the Mediterranean coasts and deserts of Libya, Tunisia, and Egypt. The United Kingdom fought to protect the oil fields of the Middle East. It also tried to defend the Suez Canal, the shortest sea route for the crucial exchange of supplies and troops with Asia. British and Commonwealth troops struck back at the Italians in December 1940, sweeping them from Egypt. But an Axis invasion of Greece drew part of the Allied force from Africa and ended the Allied advance.

Early in 1941, Hitler sent *panzer* (*PAHN tsuhr*) (tank) units trained in desert warfare to help the Italians in North Africa. German Field Marshal Erwin Rommel (*RAW muhl*) (1891-1944) led the panzer units. They were known as the *Afrikakorps (AH free kah kawr)*. Rommel's clever tactics earned him the nickname "The Desert Fox." After a series of battles in Libya, Rommel drove into Egypt. But the British again repelled the Axis forces. In May 1942, Rommel broke through into Egypt again. He threatened the port of Alexandria, the capital city of Cairo, and the vital Suez Canal. British forces led by Lieutenant General Bernard Law Montgomery (1887-1976) met Rommel at El Alamein (*ehl ah lah MAYN*) on Oct. 23, 1942. The ensuing tank battle raged until November 5 when Rommel's defeated forces withdrew. The Desert War, however, was far from over.

Allied dead in the Western Desert amounted to more than 35,000. More than 30,000 German and Italian soldiers were killed.

Hitler pressured Bulgaria, Hungary, and Romania into joining the Axis. These countries provided Germany with vast supplies of food, petroleum, and personnel. Yugoslavia's government signed an agreement with the Axis in March 1941. But the Yugoslav military rebelled and overthrew the government. An enraged Hitler ordered the young nation crushed. German troops poured into Yugoslavia on April 6. Yugoslavia surrendered on April 17. But underground resistance there remained stubborn and deadly until the end of the war.

Mussolini had tired of playing Hitler's junior partner. He wanted a victory to boost his standing. On Oct. 28, 1940, Italian forces based in Albania invaded Greece. They expected to defeat the poorly equipped Greek army easily. Though outnumbered, the Greeks fought fiercely. By December, they had driven the Italians out of Greece and had overrun part of Albania. The United Kingdom sent a small force to help the Greeks. But in April 1941, a much larger German force came to the aid of the Italians. By the end of the month, the Axis was in control. British troops withdrew to the island of Crete.

On May 20, 1941, thousands of German paratroopers descended on Crete and seized an airfield. More German troops then landed, securing

German Field Marshal Erwin Rommel (standing in jeep) led German *panzer* (tank) units trained in desert warfare to help the Italian forces in North Africa. Rommel's clever tactics with the panzer units, known as Afrikakorps, earned him the nickname "The Desert Fox."

Benito Mussolini

Benito Mussolini (*beh NEE toh moos soh LEE nee*) (1883-1945) founded fascism and ruled Italy for almost 21 years, most of that time as dictator. He dreamed of building Italy into a great empire, but he led his nation to defeat in World War II and was executed by his own people.

Mussolini was born on July 29, 1883, in Dovia (*DOH vee yuh*), near Forli (*FAWR lee*), in northeastern Italy. Mussolini served in the Italian military in 1905 and 1906 and became a local socialist leader. In 1909, he went to Trent, Austria (now Trento, Italy), and worked for a socialist newspaper. But Austrian authorities expelled him from Austria because of his revolutionary activities.

In 1914, Mussolini founded his own newspaper, *Il Popolo d'Italia,* in which he urged Italy to enter World War I (1914-1918) against Germany and Austria-Hungary. Italy entered the war in 1915, and Mussolini served in the army until he was wounded in 1917. In 1919, he founded the *Fasci di Combattimento* (Combat Groups). This movement appealed to war veterans. It supported government ownership of national resources and put the interests of Italy above all others. In 1921, Mussolini transformed the Fasci into the National Fascist Party. Armed squads called the

Black Shirts, who supported Mussolini, used violence to combat anti-Fascist groups. In 1922, the Black Shirts staged a March on Rome and forced King Victor Emmanuel III (1869-1947) to appoint Mussolini prime minister. In 1925, Mussolini declared a dictatorship. He abolished other political parties and imposed government control on industry, schools, the press, and police.

The powerful Mussolini was called *Il Duce* (*eel DOO chay*) (The Leader). Mussolini sought to make Italy a major world power and create an Italian colonial empire. He invaded and conquered Ethiopia in 1935 and 1936. But this action was condemned by the United Kingdom, France, and other countries and drove Mussolini toward an alliance with German dictator Adolf Hitler. In 1936, he joined Hitler in sending troops to fight in the Spanish Civil War in support of the rebel leader General Francisco Franco. In 1939, Italy conquered and annexed Albania.

World War II began in 1939, and France and the United Kingdom declared war on Germany. In 1940, just before France fell to Germany, Mussolini entered the war and invaded France. A few days later, France surrendered. But Mussolini's troops soon suffered serious setbacks in North Africa and Greece. They met even stronger opposition after the Soviet Union, and later the United States, joined the war against Italy and Germany.

In July 1943, the Italian government deposed Mussolini and restored authority to the king, who then had Mussolini arrested. Mussolini was rescued by German commandos and became the head of a puppet government in northern Italy. On April 27, 1945, Italians opposed to fascism captured Mussolini as he attempted to escape to Switzerland. The next day, he was shot to death.

the island. The victory gave Germany an important base in the Mediterranean.

Thousands of Allied and Axis troops died in the Balkan Campaign. The defeats in the Balkans were blows to the Allies. However, the detours into Yugoslavia and Greece were costly for Hitler, too. They delayed his invasion of the Soviet Union.

The Soviet Union and its enormous Red Army were constant threats to Hitler. He privately viewed them—and Communism itself—as Germany's chief enemy. He feared Soviet ambitions to expand in eastern Europe, while planning to expand there himself. The German dictator desired more *lebensraum* (*LAY buhns ROWM*) (living space) for his people. Hitler also wanted control of the vast wheat and oil fields of Ukraine and elsewhere within the Soviet Union. Hitler's 1939 nonaggression pact with Stalin was a stalling tactic on both their parts. It served merely to keep the Soviet Union out of the war while Germany overran western Europe.

Stalin sought to obtain more naval bases and strengthen Soviet borders. In November 1939, the Soviet Union invaded Finland. An outnumbered and outgunned Finnish army fought fiercely for five months in what came to be known as the Winter War. Finland surrendered in March 1940, giving Stalin minor territorial concessions. The much smaller Finnish Army lost about 25,000 troops killed in action. The Red Army lost about 200,000. In the summer of 1940, the Soviet Union seized the countries of Estonia, Latvia, and Lithuania along the Baltic Sea.

The length and difficulty of Stalin's Winter War with Finland helped give Hitler a low opinion of the Red Army. The Soviet Union may have had the largest army in the world at the time. But the German army was better trained, better equipped, and better led.

The German invasion of the Soviet Union, *Operation Barbarossa,*

In a surprise attack, Germany invaded the Soviet Union in June 1941. German armored and mechanized units (shown here) captured the Soviet city of Minsk as part of the invasion, code named Operation Barbarossa.

began on June 22, 1941. It started five weeks later than Hitler had intended. His generals warned of the dangers of the Russian winter. But Hitler was confident the fighting would be over before the first snowfall. Stalin ignored Allied warnings of the coming invasion. The attack took the Soviet Union by surprise.

More than 3 million German and Axis troops invaded along a 2,000-mile (3,220-kilometer) front. Germany's *Panzerkorps (PAN zehr kawr),* an armored and mechanized unit, smashed through the Soviet lines. Luftwaffe squadrons devastated the Red Air Force. In only a few weeks, the Germans killed or captured hundreds of thousands of Soviet soldiers. The Germans pushed far into Soviet territory. As the Red Army and civilians retreated, they destroyed factories, dams, railroads, and food supplies. They wanted to deprive the enemy of anything that might be useful.

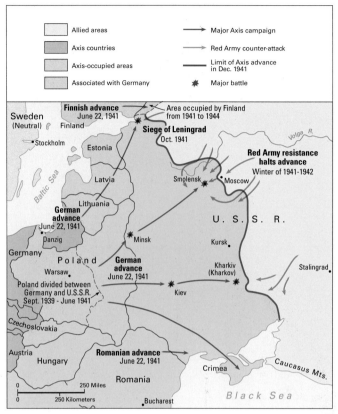

Allied areas	→ Major Axis campaign
Axis countries	→ Red Army counter-attack
Axis-occupied areas	— Limit of Axis advance in Dec. 1941
Associated with Germany	✴ Major battle

Sweden (Neutral)

Finnish advance
June 22, 1941

Area occupied by Finland from 1941 to 1944

Finland

Volga R.

Stockholm

Estonia

Siege of Leningrad
Oct. 1941

Red Army resistance
halts advance
Winter of 1941-1942

Baltic Sea

Latvia

Smolensk

Moscow

Lithuania

German
advance
June 22, 1941

U. S. S. R.

Danzig

Minsk

Kursk

Germany

P o l a n d

German
advance
June 22, 1941

Kharkiv
(Kharkov)

Stalingrad

Warsaw

Kiev

Poland divided between
Germany and U.S.S.R.
Sept. 1939 - June 1941

Czechoslovakia

Austria

Hungary

Romanian advance
June 22, 1941

Crimea

Caucasus Mts.

Romania

Black Sea

Bucharest

0   250 Miles
0   250 Kilometers

Operation Barbarossa, the German invasion of the Soviet Union, began in June 1941. German forces captured massive amounts of Soviet territory, along with millions of Red Army troops. The German advance slowed as the weather worsened later in the year. In December, the Soviets stopped the Germans short of Moscow, the Soviet capital.

Looking for the killer blow, Hitler's generals wanted to press on immediately to Moscow. Instead, Hitler sent his Panzerkorps to join the German armies heading through Ukraine toward the Crimean Peninsula on the Black Sea. While the Germans weakened their center and spent time transferring forces, Stalin reinforced. The German advance slowed. But on September 19, the Germans took the city of Kiev. It was Germany's greatest single victory of the war. Germany captured nearly 665,000 Soviet soldiers. A total of 1.5 million Soviets had been taken prisoner up to that point in the campaign. Another 700,000 had been killed. German dead had already passed 100,000.

In October, the Panzerkorps returned to the German center for the advance on Moscow. But the autumn rains had come. German tanks and artillery bogged down in the mud just 40 miles (64 kilometers) from the Russian capital. On Nov. 15, 1941, exhausted German soldiers attacked Moscow. Fresh Soviet troops from the Far East combined with the onslaught of winter to stop the Germans 20 miles (32 kilometers) from the city. The Germans had no winter clothing. Temperatures plunged to −40 °F (−40 °C). German soldiers suffered terribly. Tanks and weapons seized up. Stuck vehicles became a part of the frozen earth. As it had been in wars past, winter was once again the Soviet Union's greatest ally.

By December 1941, Operation Barbarossa had claimed the lives of 200,000 German soldiers. Thousands of Croatians, Hungarians, Italians, Romanians, and Slovaks were among them. The Red Army had already suffered hundreds of thousands killed and more than 3 million captured. The worst fighting, however, was yet to come.

Meanwhile, on the high seas, the Allied war effort depended heavily on shipments of food, military equipment and supplies, and other provisions across the Atlantic Ocean from North America. Germany tried to stop the shipments. The Allies struggled to keep the supplies coming.

Germany's surface fleet could not seriously challenge the United Kingdom's Royal Navy. But German warships attacked *merchant vessels* (commercial ships). The Royal Navy hunted down and sank such raiders one by one. The biggest operation was against the powerful German battleship *Bismarck*. In May 1941, a fleet of British warships chased, trapped, and finally sank the *Bismarck*. Afterward, Germany's large warships rarely left harbor.

The greatest threat to Allied shipping came from German submarines, called *Unterseeboote* (*OON tehr see boh tuh*) or U-boats. The U-boats prowled the Atlantic and torpedoed any Allied ships they spotted. The conquests of Norway and France gave Germany bases for its U-boats. As a defensive measure, the United Kingdom began to use a convoy system

Allied merchant ships traveled in groups called convoys escorted by warships to defend against German submarine attacks. This photo shows smoke billowing from merchant ships bombed in an Allied convoy in the North Atlantic Ocean during World War II.

in which merchant ships sailed in large groups escorted by warships.

From 1940 to 1942, Germany appeared to be winning the Battle of the Atlantic. Each month, U-boats sank thousands of tons of Allied shipping. But the Allies gradually overcame the U-boat danger. They used surface radar and an underwater detection device called *sonar* to locate German submarines. Long-range aircraft bombed U-boats as they surfaced. Shipyards in North America stepped up their production of warships to accompany convoys. Eventually, the Allies were sinking U-boats faster than Germany could replace them. After terrible losses in "Black May" 1943, the U-boat "wolf packs" retreated and regrouped. The U-boats resumed action in the fall. But they never repeated their previous success.

The Battle of the Atlantic was the longest military campaign of World War II. It lasted the length of the war. The Germans launched nearly 1,200 submarines. Of these, close to 800 were sunk. Out of about 40,000 German submariners sent into action, 28,000 never returned—the highest death rate of any armed service in the history of modern warfare. About 3,000 Allied ships sank to the bottom of the Atlantic Ocean, and more than 70,000 Allied merchant mariners, sailors, and aviators lost their lives.

Due to the battle's length, the Allies' rally in the Battle of the Atlantic coincided with their overall surge in the war. The entry of the United States into World War II came as the Allies began to chip away at Germany. The United States would make a strategic decision to focus first on the European front, which helped the Allies counter the Axis attacks.

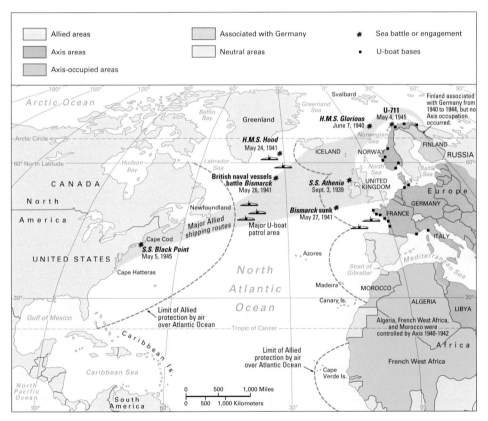

The Battle of the Atlantic lasted from the first day of World War II in 1939 until Germany surrendered in 1945. As this map shows, Allied ships were most vulnerable in the North Atlantic Ocean beyond the protection of Allied aircraft. Many German U-boats (submarines) lurked in these areas, but U-boats could strike almost anywhere.

President Franklin D. Roosevelt (right, at podium) addressed a joint session of Congress on Dec. 8, 1941, a day after Japan's surprise attack on Pearl Harbor, Hawaii. Roosevelt said December 7 was "a date which will live in infamy."

CHAPTER FOUR

The United States enters the war; Allies advance

After World War II began in 1939, United States President Franklin D. Roosevelt announced the neutrality of the United States. Canada, as part of the Commonwealth of Nations, entered the war on Sept. 10, 1939, one week after the United Kingdom.

Roosevelt and many other Americans wanted to do more to help the Allies. These people, called *interventionists,* argued that an Axis victory would endanger democracies everywhere. Roosevelt urged "all aid short of war" to nations fighting the Axis. *Isolationists,* on the other hand, thought that the United States should not interfere in European affairs. They opposed giving aid to warring nations. They accused Roosevelt of steering the nation into a war it was not prepared to fight. Most people in the United States thought the Allied cause was just. But they wanted their country to stay out of World War II.

Roosevelt hoped to contribute to the defeat of the Axis powers by equipping the Allies. Roosevelt asked his fellow Americans to become what he called "the arsenal of democracy," meaning that the United States would supply military equipment to the Allies.

The United States took several steps toward war. In November 1939, U.S. neutrality laws were changed to allow the sale of arms to warring nations—specifically the United Kingdom and France. In September 1940, the United States Navy gave the United Kingdom 50 destroyers to protect Atlantic convoys. In March 1941, with the Allies nearly broke, the United States Congress approved the Lend-Lease Act. The act permitted President Roosevelt to lend or lease raw materials, supplies, and weapons to any nation fighting the Axis. In all, 38 nations received a total of about $50 billion in aid through the Lend-Lease Act. More than half the aid went to the British Empire. About a fourth went to the Soviet Union.

Franklin D. Roosevelt and World War II

Franklin Delano Roosevelt (*FRANK lihn DEHL uh noh ROH zuh vehlt*) (1882-1945) was the 32nd president of the United States. Roosevelt, a Democrat, held the office from 1933 to 1945. He was elected president four times and occupied the White House for over 12 years—longer than any other president in American history. Roosevelt led the United States through two of the greatest crises in the country's history: the Great Depression of the 1930's and World War II.

During the Depression, the United States and countries throughout the world struggled with high unemployment and declining business activity. Roosevelt led an ambitious government program—known as the New Deal—to help relieve economic distress. During World War II, he led the nation in a successful military operation that had farther-reaching consequences than any other war effort in history. Roosevelt died in 1945, three months after the start of his fourth term. Since that time, historians have often ranked him, along with George Washington and Abraham Lincoln, as one of the nation's greatest presidents.

In the months following Roosevelt's third inauguration, the nation edged closer to war. On March 11, 1941, Congress passed the Lend-Lease Act. The law authorized the U.S. government to provide war supplies to any nation that the president deemed vital to the nation's security.

In August 1941, Roosevelt met British Prime Minister Winston Churchill on a cruiser anchored off the province of Newfoundland (now Newfoundland and Labrador), Canada. The two men adopted a declaration that became known as the Atlantic Charter. They pledged not to seek gains, "territorial or otherwise"; to respect the right of every nation to choose its own form of government; to guarantee freedom of the seas; and to conduct peaceful world trade.

President Roosevelt signs the declaration of war against Germany during World War II. Senator Thomas Connally of Texas stands by holding a watch to mark the exact time of the declaration.

On Dec. 7, 1941, U.S. Secretary of State Cordell Hull (1871-1955) met with two Japanese diplomats. While they talked, Japanese planes launched a surprise attack on the U.S. Pacific Fleet, which lay at anchor in Pearl Harbor, Hawaii. Japanese leaders hoped to knock out the Pacific Fleet so that it could not block Japan's expansion in Asia. The Pearl Harbor attack destroyed or damaged many U.S. ships and aircraft and killed nearly 2,400 Americans.

President Roosevelt addressed Congress the next day. He said that December 7 was "a date which will live in infamy." The United States declared war against Japan on December 8. Three days later, on December 11, Germany and Italy declared war on the United States. The United

States then declared war on those countries.

During the war, Roosevelt traveled outside the United States a number of times for conferences with Allied leaders. He became the first U.S. president to leave the country during wartime. Early in 1943, he met with Churchill in Casablanca, Morocco. The two leaders announced that they would accept only unconditional surrender by the Axis nations. In other conferences, Roosevelt discussed problems of war and peace with both Churchill and Premier Joseph Stalin of the Soviet Union. Roosevelt, Churchill, and Stalin came to be known as the "Big Three." Roosevelt also conferred with Generalissimo Chiang Kai-shek of China in 1943.

In November 1943, the Big Three met at Tehran, Iran. During and after this conference, Roosevelt worked to get Churchill and Stalin to agree on major war aims. At Tehran, he refused to have lunch with Churchill before meeting with Stalin. The president did not want Stalin to think he and Churchill had made a separate agreement. Still, Stalin distrusted his allies' intentions and rarely consulted them.

Roosevelt's domestic leadership was critical to the war effort. His radio "fireside chats" helped reassure the nation and drive both the military and civilians to meet ambitious wartime goals. After a sluggish start, American war industries achieved astonishing feats, producing many of the guns, tanks, planes, and ships used by the Allied forces. In the end, this productivity was perhaps the single most important contribution to victory made by the United States.

The most dramatic development on the home front was the economic recovery, which was driven by the huge increase in government spending for war purposes. The production of war materials provided so many jobs that the U.S. unemployment rate fell to about 1 percent in 1944.

Congress granted Roosevelt broad authority to manage the military aspects of the war. But on matters not directly related to war conduct,

"Fireside chats" became a regular feature of Roosevelt's presidency. These informal radio reports to the American people enabled Roosevelt to gain widespread support for his programs.

Roosevelt was frequently at odds with lawmakers, including members of his own party. The conservative coalition of Republicans and southern Democrats in Congress chipped away at the remaining programs of the New Deal.

In 1944, lawmakers from both parties came together to pass, by unanimous votes, the first GI Bill, the Servicemen's Readjustment Act, for veterans of World War II. The measure guaranteed education assistance, medical benefits, unemployment insurance, and low-interest home loans to veterans of the war. Of the many laws enacted during the Roosevelt presidency, the GI Bill probably ranked second only to the Social Security Act in its long-term impact on the economy.

Roosevelt generally supported civil rights. In February 1942, however, he approved measures against Japanese Americans that many people now consider unnecessary and discriminatory. The president yielded to political pressure and ordered the *internment* (confinement) of more than 110,000 people of Japanese ancestry in the United States. At that time, many Americans viewed people of Japanese descent as potentially dangerous and disloyal. With little warning, the U.S. government forced people to leave their homes and live in camps. A government commission later concluded that the internment was the result of racism, war hysteria, and poor leadership.

Roosevelt created a Fair Employment Practices Commission (FEPC) to prevent defense industries and the federal government from treating workers unfairly because of their race. But fearing a white backlash that might endanger the war effort, he declined to end *segregation* (separation of the races) in the armed services.

Roosevelt often claimed that he yearned to retire to his home in Hyde Park, New York. He struggled with his health, and he looked tired and pale. But with the war still in progress, he continued his presidency into a fourth term.

Just days after his fourth inauguration, Roosevelt met Churchill and Stalin at Yalta, a resort on the Black Sea in the southern Soviet Union. On Feb. 11, 1945, the three leaders issued the Declaration on Liberated Europe, which repeated the principles of the Atlantic Charter and the Casablanca conferences. The leaders mapped the final assault against the Germans and set out a plan for the postwar occupation of Germany. They also planned a meeting in San Francisco to lay the foundations for the United Nations (UN). In a secret agreement, the Soviet Union promised to enter the war against Japan within three months after the surrender of Germany. In return, the Soviet Union was to receive the Kuril

During the war, Roosevelt traveled overseas several times to confer with Allied leaders. Here, he is shown riding in a jeep in Sicily with Allied Commander Dwight D. Eisenhower.

(*KOO rihl*) Islands and other areas. Critics later charged that Roosevelt had been cheated by Stalin.

On March 1, while reporting to Congress on the Yalta meeting, Roosevelt made a rare public reference to the paralysis of his legs, which resulted from him catching polio in 1921. "I hope that you will pardon me for this unusual posture of sitting down," he said, but "it makes it a lot easier for me not to have to carry about 10 pounds of steel around at the bottom of my legs."

By the spring of 1945, the war in Europe was nearing an end, and the war in the Pacific was going well. In March, Roosevelt visited "the Little White House," his long-time retreat in Warm Springs, Georgia. Eleanor, his wife, (1884-1962) who maintained a demanding schedule as First Lady, did not accompany him on the trip. Joining him instead were several staff members and cousins Laura Delano and Margaret (also known as Daisy) Suckley. Lucy Mercer Rutherfurd, the woman whom he had loved years earlier, arrived on April 9. The two had seen each other from time to time during the 1940's, especially since the death of Lucy's husband the year before.

By Thursday, April 12, Roosevelt seemed to have regained some of his strength. He spent the morning reading and chatting with his cousins and Lucy Rutherfurd. At noon, Elizabeth Shoumatoff, a portrait artist, arrived to work on a watercolor painting of the president. Shortly after 1 p.m., he passed his hand over his forehead several times. "I have a terrific headache," he said softly. He then slumped forward in his chair. By the time his doctor arrived, he was unconscious and breathing heavily. Soon thereafter, his breathing stopped.

At 3:35 p.m., the doctor pronounced Roosevelt dead of a *cerebral hemorrhage* (bleeding from a broken blood vessel in the brain). As news of his death spread, a crowd, silent with grief, gathered in front of the White House. Millions of people in all parts of the world mourned the dead president.

Roosevelt was buried at Hyde Park. His home and library there have been set aside as the Franklin D. Roosevelt National Historic Site. In 1997, the Franklin Delano Roosevelt Memorial was dedicated on the National Mall in Washington, D.C.

Pearl Harbor and the Big Three

Japan's expansion in Southeast Asia troubled the United States. In September 1940, as Japanese troops occupied northern Indochina, the United States cut off vital exports to Japan. Japanese industries relied

Explosions ripped through the USS *Shaw* after it was hit by Japanese bombs during the attack on Pearl Harbor, Hawaii, on Dec. 7, 1941. The sneak attack killed 2,400 Americans; sank several U.S. ships, including four battleships; and brought the United States into World War II.

heavily on petroleum, scrap metal, and other raw materials from the United States. After Japan seized the rest of Indochina in 1941, Roosevelt barred the withdrawal of Japanese funds from American banks.

General Hideki Tojo (*hee deh kee toh joh*) (1884-1948) became prime minister of Japan in October 1941. Tojo and Japan's other military leaders realized that only the United States Navy had the power to block Japan's expansion in Asia. They decided to cripple the U.S. Pacific Fleet with one forceful blow.

On Dec. 7, 1941, the Japanese launched a surprise attack upon the U.S. Pacific Fleet at Pearl Harbor, Hawaii. Two waves of Japanese warplanes sank several U.S. ships, including four battleships. They also destroyed more than 180 U.S. aircraft. The Japanese killed 2,400 Americans, but lost only about 100 of their own troops. The attack was a success. But bringing the United States into the war would prove disastrous for the Japanese Empire and its citizens.

The United States, Canada, and the United Kingdom declared war on Japan on Dec. 8, 1941. Germany and Italy declared war on the United States three days later, on December 11. The world was now truly a world at war.

Soviet forces held off the German advance in eastern Europe in 1942. The Soviets won a major victory at Stalingrad (now Volgograd) in 1943.

A U.S. government poster (right) reminded Americans of the event that plunged them into war—Japan's attack on Pearl Harbor. All warring nations used propaganda techniques to stir patriotism.

...we here highly resolve that these dead shall not have died in vain...

REMEMBER DEC. 7th!

The Allies invaded North Africa in 1942 and forced Italy to surrender the next year. In 1944, Allied troops swarmed into France in the largest seaborne invasion in history. Allied attacks from the east and the west forced Germany to surrender in 1945.

Churchill, Roosevelt, and Stalin, the leaders of the three major Allied powers, met in three major conferences during World War II. Churchill and Roosevelt conferred frequently on overall strategy. Stalin, however, directed the Soviet war effort, but rarely consulted with Churchill and Roosevelt.

The main wartime disagreement among the Big Three concerned an Allied invasion of western Europe. Stalin constantly urged Roosevelt and Churchill to open a second fighting front in western Europe and thus draw German troops from the Soviet front. Both Roosevelt and Churchill supported the idea. But they disagreed on where and when to invade. The Americans wanted to land in northern France as soon as possible. The British argued that an invasion of France before the Allies were fully prepared would be disastrous. Instead, Churchill favored invading Italy first. His view won out.

At a meeting in August 1941, Roosevelt and Churchill issued the Atlantic Charter, stating the postwar aims of the United States and the United Kingdom. After the Japanese attacked Pearl Harbor, Roosevelt and Churchill conferred in Washington, D.C. The two leaders felt that Germany was a nearer and more dangerous enemy than Japan. They decided to concentrate on defeating Germany first.

Roosevelt and Churchill met again in January 1943. At the conference in Casablanca, Morocco, they agreed to invade the Mediterranean island of Sicily after driving the Germans and Italians from northern Africa. Roosevelt announced that the Allies would accept only a complete surrender from the Axis powers. Churchill supported him.

Roosevelt and Churchill first met with Stalin in November 1943 in Tehran, Iran. The Big Three discussed plans for a joint British and American invasion of France in the spring of 1944. They did not meet again until Germany neared collapse. In February 1945, Roosevelt, Churchill, and Stalin gathered at Yalta, a Soviet city on the Crimean Peninsula. They agreed that their countries would each occupy a zone of Germany after the war. France was to occupy a fourth zone. Roosevelt died on April 12, 1945, less than one month before the end of the war in Europe.

The Soviet Red Army struck back at the Germans outside Moscow on Dec. 5, 1941. The Soviets pushed the invaders back about 100 miles (160 kilometers). But as the weather broke in the spring of 1942, the Germans regrouped and prepared for a summer offensive—*Operation Blue.* Hitler was now personally directing the war. He bolstered his battered armies with divisions from Hungary, Italy, Romania, Slovakia, and Spain.

Leaders of the "Big Three" major Allied powers, (from left) Soviet leader Joseph Stalin, U.S. President Franklin Roosevelt, and British Prime Minister Winston Churchill, met in Tehran, Iran, in late 1943.

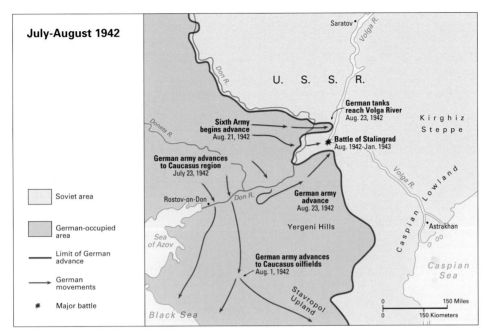

July-August 1942

Saratov

Volga R.

U. S. S. R.

Don R.

German tanks
reach Volga River
Aug. 23, 1942

Kirghiz
Steppe

Donets R.

Sixth Army
begins advance
Aug. 21, 1942

Battle of Stalingrad
Aug. 1942-Jan. 1943

German army advances
to Caucasus region
July 23, 1942

Volga R.

Lowland

Rostov-on-Don

Don R.

German army
advance
Aug. 23, 1942

Caspian

Astrakhan

Yergeni Hills

Sea
of Azov

German army advances
to Caucasus oilfields
Aug. 1, 1942

Caspian
Sea

Stavropol
Upland

Black Sea

Soviet area	
German-occupied area	
Limit of German advance	
German movements	
Major battle	

0   150 Miles

0   150 Kiometers

German troops forced their way into Stalingrad in August 1942.
The Soviet Red Army fought ferociously but suffered tremendous
losses. German troops captured most of Stalingrad, forcing the
Soviets into small pockets along the Volga River.

The combined Axis forces overran the Crimean Peninsula and headed
eastward toward the rich oil fields in the Caucasus. Hitler ordered
General Friedrich von Paulus to take the city of Stalingrad. About 1
million German soldiers poured into the city. The Soviets rose to meet
them. Stalin had ordered, "Not one step back." The savage battle for
Stalingrad began in September and dragged through the autumn. The
Germans took most of the city but could not hold it. Neighborhoods, city
blocks, even individual buildings were fought over for days or weeks.
Thousands of people died. Then the same buildings were fought over
again.

Paulus's losses mounted. The German commander repeatedly asked

Germany's defeat at Stalingrad (above) ended the Nazis eastward advance into the Soviet Union. Hitler sent in 1 million soldiers to take the city, but they could not break through the Soviet lines.

for permission to pull out. Hitler repeatedly refused. Soviet troops counterattacked in mid-November, eventually trapping Paulus's army. The Luftwaffe attempted to resupply the army by air. But it was too little, too late. Each day, thousands of German soldiers froze, starved to death, or died of disease. On Feb. 2, 1943, after months of suffering, the last German troops in Stalingrad surrendered.

The Battle of Stalingrad halted Germany's eastward advance. It marked a turning point in the war as the advantage swung to the Soviets. It was one of the largest battles in human history. Its cost was horrific. About 450,000 Axis troops were killed. The Soviets lost at least 500,000 soldiers and hundreds of thousands of civilians.

In September 1941, the northern group of German armies surrounded the Russian city of Leningrad (now St. Petersburg). German warplanes and artillery bombarded the city. Nearly all supplies were cut off. The more than 2 million citizens and soldiers of Leningrad held out. They suffered through winters without electric power. They endured shortages of water, food, and medicine. All the while, they suffered bombardment by German artillery.

The Battle of El Alamein (*ehl ah la MAYN*) in late 1942, like Stalingrad, marked a turning point in the war. The Axis never again attacked in North Africa. On Nov. 8, 1942, Allied troops commanded by Lieutenant General Dwight D. Eisenhower (1890-1969) of the U.S. Army landed in Algeria and Morocco. Vichy French forces initially resisted the Ameri-

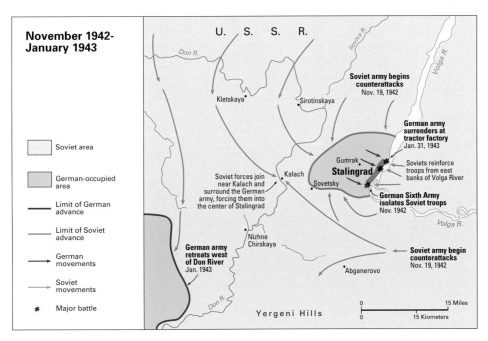

In November 1942, a massive Soviet counterattack split the German forces in two. The main German force withdrew to the west, abandoning an entire German army in Stalingrad.

Siege of Leningrad

The Siege of Leningrad was a blockade of the city of Leningrad in the Soviet Union by German and Finnish troops during World War II. Leningrad is now St. Petersburg, Russia. The siege lasted 872 days, from September 1941 to January 1944. Historians estimate that about 1.7 million Soviet people, including military personnel and civilians, may have died in and around Leningrad during the siege. But the enemy failed to capture the city. Leningrad's defense was a critical event in the war. Had the city fallen, the Germans could have exerted more pressure on the Soviet capital, Moscow, and possibly conquered it.

Germany attacked the Soviet Union in June 1941. Nazi dictator Adolf Hitler ordered the destruction of Leningrad, an important center for industry and weapons production. By September 8, the blockade was complete. The only connection that Leningrad maintained with the rest of the Soviet Union was across nearby Lake Ladoga (*LAH duh guh*), which German aircraft patrolled.

German artillery and aircraft bombarded Leningrad through-

German artillery and aircraft bombarded Leningrad (left), an important center for industry and weapons production in the Soviet Union. German dictator Adolf Hitler ordered the destruction of Leningrad during a blockade of the city by German troops during World War II.

out the siege. The blockade produced severe shortages of fuel, food, and raw materials. During the winter and spring of 1941-1942, nearly 1 million Leningraders died from a combination of starvation and extreme cold. Bread was the only food that was regularly available, and the daily bread ration dropped as low as about 4.5 ounces (125 grams) for nonworkers and children. The temperature fell to – 40 °F (– 40 °C) in early 1942. Because of the frigid weather, however, Lake Ladoga froze, enabling the Soviets to build roads

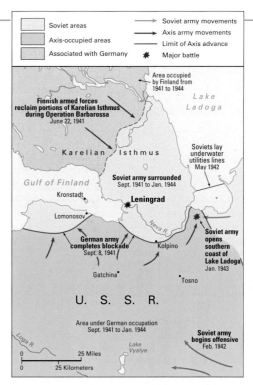

The Siege of Leningrad lasted from September 1941 until January 1944. The city received a trickle of supplies through, beneath, and over Lake Ladoga to the east. The dangerous wintertime road over the frozen lake became known as the *Doroga Zhizni,* or *Road of Life.*

across the ice. Trucks delivered food to the city by means of the roads, and hundreds of thousands of starving Leningraders were evacuated over them.

In January 1943, the Soviet Red Army retook enough land along Lake Ladoga's southern coast to extend a rail line into the city. But the siege continued until Jan. 27, 1944, when German troops retreated before the advancing Red Army.

cans. But within two days, they had joined the Allied cause.

The Allies hoped to advance rapidly into Tunisia and cut off the Axis forces from their home bases in Italy and Sicily. But Axis troops moved faster and seized Tunisia first. There, German Field Marshal Erwin Rommel prepared for battle. The first major clash between American and German combat troops was in mid-February during the fight for Kasserine (*KAH suh REEN*) Pass. Rommel defeated the inexperienced Americans. But thereafter, the Allies steadily closed in. Rommel returned to Germany. The last Axis forces in North Africa surrendered in May—about 250,000 of them. The Allies had saved the oil fields of the Middle East. They also sustained the supply route to Asia and cleared a path for the invasions of Sicily and Italy.

Axis deaths in the Tunisian Campaign numbered over 14,000. The British, Americans, and French lost over 10,000 troops.

The Allies planned to invade the Italian island of Sicily after driving the Axis forces out of northern Africa. Axis planes had bombed Allied ships in the Mediterranean Sea from bases in Sicily. The Allies wanted to make the Mediterranean safe for their ships. They also hoped that an invasion of Sicily might knock a war-weary Italy out of the war.

Allied forces under Eisenhower landed along Sicily's south coast on July 10, 1943. For 38 days, they engaged in bitter fighting with the enemy over rugged terrain. The last Germans left Sicily on August 17.

B-17 Flying Fortress and the air war

Before World War II began, many aviation experts claimed the long-range *bomber* (airplane used to drop explosives) was the most advanced weapon in the world. They believed that bombers could wipe out cities and industries. In this way, bombing could destroy an enemy's desire and ability to go on fighting. The theory was tested during World War II.

A United States 8th Air Force B-17 Flying Fortress leaves a German fighter aircraft plant in flames following a bombing raid in 1943.

By May 1941, Germany's bombing of the United Kingdom had largely stopped. But RAF bombers pounded Germany until the end of the war. At first, the bombing was costly and ineffective. British losses were heavy. RAF Bomber Command relied on *area bombing*. Area bombing involved dropping many bombs on an area without pinpointing targets. Bomber Command also favored nighttime raids. Night raids were safer than daytime raids, but bombers too often missed their targets in the

"Rosie the Riveter" became the humorous yet respectful name for the millions of American women who worked in defense plants during World War II. This "Rosie" worked on an airplane assembly line.

dark. In 1942, the United Kingdom turned to *saturation bombing* of German cities. Such bombing involved dropping enough bombs to totally destroy the target area. A massive group of more than 1,000 aircraft battered the railyards and city of Cologne on May 30, 1942. Bomber Command continued its nighttime raids on German cities to the end of the war. It made 35 raids on Berlin alone.

Meanwhile, the U.S. Army Air Forces had arrived. They joined the air campaign against Germany in 1942. The American B-17 bomber carried a better bombsight than British planes. B-17's were known as Flying Fortresses because of their heavy armor and many guns. They could take much punishment. For those reasons, the Americans favored *precision bombing*. It involved placing bombs with a high degree of accuracy. The Americans directed their bombing at mostly industrial and military targets and carried out their bombing raids during the day.

The B-17 Flying Fortress was a heavy military airplane used by the United States and its allies during World War II. It was a four-engine bomber made by the Boeing Company. *B* is the U.S. military's designation for a bomber. The plane was called the *Flying Fortress* because of its many machine guns used for defense against enemy aircraft. The B-17 became a lasting symbol of American air power.

The B-17 had a large tailfin that helped it maneuver in the thin air of high altitudes. The bomber carried as many as 13 heavy machine guns, 10 crew members, and up to 17,600 pounds (7,983 kilograms) of bombs. The airplane flew at a top speed of about 300 miles (480 kilometers) per hour. It could reach a maximum altitude of around 36,000 feet (11,000 meters).

The U.S. Army tested the first B-17's in 1935. They entered World War II combat with the United Kingdom's Royal Air Force in July 1941. When the United States entered the war in December, the B-17 (along with the

B-24 Liberator) became the backbone of its heavy bomber groups.

Most B-17's were used in daylight bombing raids against enemy targets in Europe. Although the bombers' guns brought down many enemy planes, large numbers of Flying Fortresses failed to return from their missions. The B-17's that flew from England sometimes left the range of the fighter planes that accompanied them, leaving the bombers vulnerable to attack. Eventually, such fighter planes as the P-51 Mustang developed the range to escort the bombers during an entire mission.

Over the course of the war, American and British bombers dropped more than 2.7 million tons (2.45 million metric tons) of explosives onto European targets. Nearly 160,000 Allied aviators were killed in the bombing campaign. About 500,000 German civilians also died.

Germany's air defenses rapidly improved during World War II. The Germans used radar to spot incoming bombers. They used fighter planes and antiaircraft guns, called *flak,* to shoot them down. In 1944, Germany introduced the first jet fighter, the Messerschmitt (*MEHS uhr SCHMIHT*) Me 262. The plane was known as the *Schwalbe (SHWAHL buh)* (Swallow). The Swallow easily overtook the propeller-driven fighters of the Allies. Also in 1944, Germany used the first guided missiles against the United Kingdom. The V-1 and V-2 missiles caused great damage and took many lives. But these innovative weapons were too few and came too late to affect the war's outcome.

From January 1943 until Germany's surrender in May 1945, B-17's pounded enemy targets throughout Europe. Hundreds of Flying Fortresses routinely took part in each mission. Of the more than 12,000 B-17's built, nearly 5,000 were lost in combat.

Despite the bombardment, German industries continued to increase production. German morale failed to crack. The air war achieved its goals only during the last 10 months of World War II. In that time, nearly

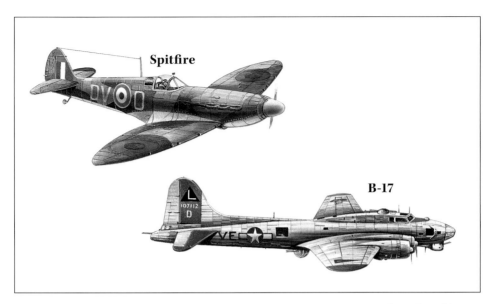

This illustration shows two airplanes—the Spitfire and the B-17—that played key roles in World War II. The Spitfire was an outstanding British fighter plane. Spitfires were noted for their speed, ability to make tight turns, and rapid climbing rate. They could outmaneuver most German fighters. In 1940, Spitfires helped defeat Germany in the Battle of Britain. A Spitfire IA is shown here. The B-17 was a widely used United States bomber. B-17's became famous for daytime raids over Germany. They were called Flying Fortresses because of their heavy armor and many guns. The B-17G, shown here, carried 13 machine guns.

three times as many bombs fell on Germany as in all the rest of the war. By the end of the war, Germany's cities lay in ruins. Its factories, refineries, railroads, and canals had nearly ceased to operate.

D-Day and the Allied advance

Mussolini fell from power on July 25, 1943. The Italian government imprisoned him. But German commandos later rescued the former dictator. Italy's new prime minister, Field Marshal Pietro Badoglio (*PYEH troh bah DAW lyoh*) (1871-1956), began secret peace talks with the Allies. Badoglio hoped to prevent Italy from becoming a battleground.

This illustration shows two military vehicles—the DUKW and the tank—that played significant roles in World War II. The DUKW, nicknamed "Duck," was an American six-wheeled truck that traveled over water and land. Ducks carried men and supplies from transport ships to enemy shores in amphibious (seaborne) landings. They were first used in the invasion of Sicily in July 1943. The tank played a key combat role in the war. In early victories, Germany massed its tanks and smashed through enemy battle lines in surprise attacks. The German Tiger heavy tank (shown here) could outgun almost all Allied tanks.

Italy surrendered on September 3. But Field Marshal Albert Kesselring (1885-1960), Germany's commander in the Mediterranean region, was determined to fight the Allies for control of Italy.

Allied forces led by U.S. Army Lieutenant General Mark W. Clark (1896-1984) landed at Salerno, Italy, on Sept. 9, 1943. It was a struggle just to stay ashore. Another Allied force had already landed farther south. The Allies struggled up the Italian Peninsula in a series of head-on assaults against well-defended German positions. By early November, the Allies had reached the Gustav Line, which was Germany's formidable defensive line about 75 miles (120 kilometers) south of Rome. Repeated Allied assaults on Cassino (*kuh SEE noh*) resulted in some of the most brutal fighting of World War II. The Gustav Line held.

In January 1944, the Allies landed at Anzio (*AHN see oh*), west of Cassino, in an effort to attack the Germans from behind. However, German forces kept the Allies pinned down on the beaches at Anzio for four months.

The Allies finally broke through German defenses in Italy in May 1944. Rome fell on June 4. The Germans held their positions in northern Italy through the fall and winter. But in the spring, the Allies swept toward the Alps. Italian resistance fighters captured Mussolini on April 27, 1945. They shot him on April 28. German forces in Italy finally surrendered on May 2. About 70,000 Allied soldiers died taking Italy. Some 48,000 Germans died defending it.

Soon after the evacuation of Dunkerque in

The Allied landings at Anzio in 1944 surprised the defending German troops. Allied forces quickly secured the port of Anzio and pushed inland. The Germans recovered, however, and stopped the Allied advance. Bitter fighting raged near Anzio for the next few months.

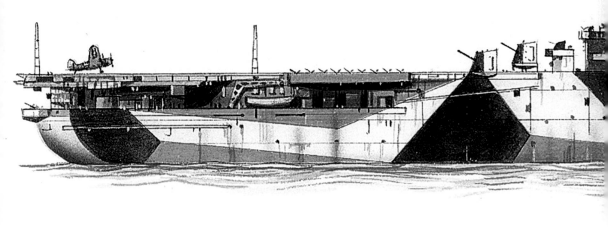

1940, the United Kingdom started to plan a return to France. In 1942, the United States and the United Kingdom began to discuss a large-scale invasion across the English Channel. To test the German defenses, the Allies raided the French port of Dieppe (*dee EHP*) in August 1942. The mostly Canadian landing force suffered disastrous losses. The Allies learned hard lessons at Dieppe. Among the lessons was that landing on open beaches had a better chance of success than landing in a port.

Throughout 1943, preparations moved ahead for an invasion of northern France the following year. The invasion plan received the code name *Operation Overlord.* Huge amounts of equipment and great numbers of troops massed in southern England. General Eisenhower, as supreme commander of the Allied forces, directed the invasion.

The Germans expected an Allied invasion along the north coast of France in 1944. But they were unsure where. A chain of fortifications, which the Germans called the Atlantic Wall, ran along the coast. Hitler

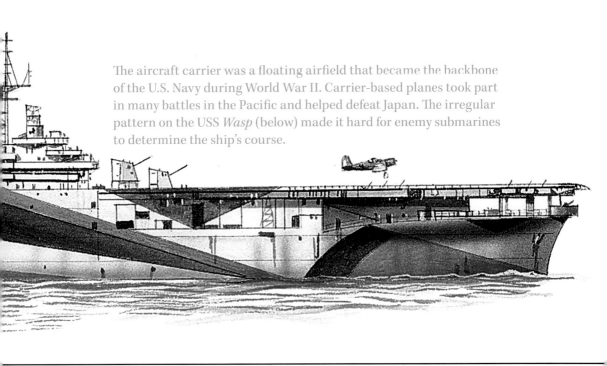

The aircraft carrier was a floating airfield that became the backbone of the U.S. Navy during World War II. Carrier-based planes took part in many battles in the Pacific and helped defeat Japan. The irregular pattern on the USS *Wasp* (below) made it hard for enemy submarines to determine the ship's course.

placed Erwin Rommel in charge of strengthening German defenses along the English Channel. Rommel brought in artillery. He placed explosive mines in the water and on the beaches. He also strung up barbed wire. The Germans concentrated their troops near Calais (*KAL ay*), at the narrowest part of the English Channel. But the Allies planned to land farther west, in a region of northern France called Normandy.

Eisenhower chose Monday, June 5, 1944, as D-Day—the date of the Normandy invasion. However, rough seas forced him to postpone until June 6. During the night, thousands of ships carrying landing craft and more than 130,000 landing troops crossed the channel. Minesweepers had gone ahead to clear the water. In addition, about 23,000 paratroopers opened fire on the beaches. At 6:30 a.m., soldiers from the United States, the United Kingdom, Canada, and France stormed ashore. They landed on a 60-mile (100-kilometer) front. It was the largest seaborne invasion in history.

Dwight D. Eisenhower during World War II

Dwight David Eisenhower (1890-1969), leader of the victorious Allied forces in Europe in World War II, rode a wave of popularity as a war hero to become president of the United States. Eisenhower had more than 30 years of military experience when he was elected chief executive in 1952, but he was remarkably unmilitary as president. He believed an effective leader inspired others to cooperate and to use their own talents to the fullest.

World War II began in 1939. Germany—later joined by Italy, Japan, and other Axis powers—fought the Allies, which included the United Kingdom, France, and later the Soviet Union and the United States. In 1940, the United States began to build up its military forces in case it was drawn into the war.

The United States entered World War II in December 1941, after Japan attacked the U.S. naval base at Pearl Harbor, Hawaii. Eisenhower went to Washington, D.C., to serve in the Army's war plans division. In June 1942, he was named commanding general of U.S. forces in the European Theater of Operations.

Eisenhower also was named commander of Allied forces organized to invade North Africa. The invasion began in November 1942 and resulted in the recapture of the region from German and Italian forces. After a series of promotions, in February 1943 Eisenhower was promoted to the rank of four-star general, then the highest in the Army. Later that year, he organized the Allied invasions of Sicily and Italy. In all these campaigns, he worked to create unity among commanders from different nations, many of whom were stubborn and outspoken.

In 1943, the United States and the United Kingdom set up a combined staff to plan the Allied invasion of German-occupied Europe. U.S. President Franklin D. Roosevelt named Eisenhower supreme commander of the Allied Expeditionary Force in Europe.

The Allies planned to cross the English Channel in early June 1944 and to invade the region of Normandy, in northern France. The plan was called Operation Overlord. Eisenhower set up headquarters near London and began the enormous responsibility and task of planning the invasion. He had to coordinate the armies and navies of the United States, the United Kingdom, and the other Allies to ensure that they worked smoothly as one force.

Eisenhower ordered the invasion to begin early on June 6, 1944, a day that became known as D-Day. By nightfall, the Allies had a firm hold on the beaches of Normandy. After 11 more months of bloody fighting, Germany surrendered on May 7, 1945.

As U.S. president, Eisenhower's broad grin and friendly manner could put almost anyone at ease. People throughout the world loved the tall, bald-headed man they fondly called "Ike." Eisenhower faced many hard decisions as president. Communist threats in Asia, Africa, and Latin America caused a series of crises. Eisenhower made little progress in reducing tensions. Yet, the soldier in the White House helped keep the world at peace.

On June 5, 1944, on the eve of the D-Day invasion of Normandy, in northern France, General Dwight D. Eisenhower (above) wished paratroopers luck before they dropped behind German lines. Eisenhower served for more than 30 years in the military before being elected president of the United States.

D-Day took the Germans by surprise. They responded fiercely. At one landing site, code-named Omaha Beach, U.S. troops came under heavy fire and barely managed to stay ashore. Nevertheless, all five Allied landing beaches were secure by the end of D-Day. The Allies soon had an artificial harbor in place for unloading more troops and supplies. A pipeline carried fuel across the channel. By the end of June 1944, about 1 million Allied troops had reached France.

The Allied forces advanced slowly. The Americans struggled westward to capture the port of Cherbourg (*SHAIR boorg*). It fell on June 27. On July

18, British and Canadian soldiers finally captured Caen (*kahn*), which the British had hoped to capture on D-Day. On July 25, Allied bombers blasted a gap in the German front near St.-Lo, about 50 miles (80 kilometers) southeast of Cherbourg. The U.S. Third Army under Lieutenant General George S. Patton plowed through the hole. The battlefield had opened up. During August, the Allies cleared the Germans out of most of northwestern France. Allied bombers hounded the retreating Germans. More than 50,000 Allied troops and aviators died in the Battle of Normandy. Tens of thousands of Germans also lost their lives.

Patton's army rolled eastward toward Paris. On Aug. 19, 1944, Parisians rose up against the occupying German forces. Resistance fighters battled the Germans street by street. American and Free French forces

American General George S. Patton makes a salute at the famous Paris landmark, the Arc de Triomphe, a memorial to French armies, while in the French capital during World War II. Patton commanded the Third Army for the French campaign and helped the Allies clear the Germans out of northwestern France.

liberated Paris on August 25.

In mid-August 1944, Allied forces landed in southern France. They moved rapidly up the Rhône (*rohn*) River Valley. Meanwhile, Patton raced eastward through the region of Lorraine (*loh RAYN*) toward the German border and the Rhine (*ryn*) River. In late August, his tanks ran out of fuel. To the north, British forces led by Montgomery, now a field marshal, swept into Belgium and captured Antwerp (*ANT wuhrp*) on September 4. The Allies planned a daring operation, code-named *Market Garden,* to carry them across the Rhine. On September 17, about 35,000 airborne soldiers began dropping behind German lines to seize bridges in the Netherlands. Additional troops invaded by land. But poor plan-

Hitting the beach, Allied infantrymen swarmed ashore along the Normandy coast of northern France on D-Day—June 6, 1944. It was the largest seaborne invasion in history. Hitler had boasted that German defenses along the coast could resist any attack. But he was wrong.

ning and bad weather hampered the operation. It ended in failure. Another path to Germany would have to be found.

Germany's generals knew they were beaten. But Hitler pulled his resources together for one more assault. On Dec. 16, 1944, German troops surprised and overwhelmed the Americans in the Ardennes Forest in Belgium and Luxembourg. However, the Germans lacked the troops and fuel to turn their thrust into a breakthrough. Within two weeks, the Americans stopped the German advance near the Meuse (*myooz*) River in Belgium.

The Ardennes offensive is known as the Battle of the Bulge because of the bulging shape of the battleground on a map. It was the bloodiest battle for the Americans in World War II. About 80,000 Americans were killed, wounded, captured, or missing. The campaigns from September 1944 to January 1945 resulted in tens of thousands of Allied and German soldiers dead. The troops and armor lost in Hitler's desperate attack in the Ardennes left Germany with little to defend itself. The end was near, but the killing would go on.

More soldiers died fighting on the Eastern Front—about 10 million—than on all other fronts combined. In 1943, the bloodletting at Stalingrad ended Germany's progress in eastern Europe. Germany could not

Soviet forces (shown here) beat back the German armies in brutal fighting to defend the Russian city of Stalingrad during World War II. German and Soviet units fought over neighborhoods, city blocks, even individual buildings for days or weeks until the German troops surrendered in early 1943.

sustain such losses. But the Soviet Union could. After January 1943, the Red Army steadily shoved the Germans back. Soviet forces had improved. They outnumbered the opposing German armies. Supplies poured into the Soviet Union from the United Kingdom and the United States. Soviet factories had also ramped up their wartime production.

Nevertheless, the German army returned to the offensive in July 1943 near the Soviet city of Kursk. There, they massed an assault against superior Soviet forces. For more than two weeks, over 2 million soldiers slaughtered one another in brutal fighting. On July 12, about 800 tanks

clashed at Prokhorovka. After the combined deaths of over 300,000 troops, the Red Army held the ground. Hitler finally called off the attack to turn his attention to the Allied invasion of Sicily.

Soviet troops moved slowly forward during the summer and fall of 1943. In January 1944, a Soviet offensive ended the siege of Leningrad. In June, soon after the Normandy invasion, Stalin's armies attacked along a 450-mile (720-kilometer) front in the east. By late July, Soviet troops had reached the outskirts of Warsaw. Poland's Home Army rose up against German forces in Warsaw on August 1. But Soviet troops refused to come to Poland's aid. Stalin permitted the Germans to destroy the Home Army. It might have resisted his plans to set up a Communist government in Poland after the war. The Warsaw uprising lasted two months. More than 200,000 Poles were killed. Soviet forces entered Warsaw in January 1945.

A German soldier (right) guards captured Polish resistance fighters during Nazi Germany's occupation of Warsaw, Poland, in 1944.

Soviet troops celebrate in Vienna, Austria, in April 1945 after liberating the capital city from the Germans.

Meanwhile, Soviet troops drove into Romania and Bulgaria. The Germans pulled out of Greece and Yugoslavia in the fall of 1944. But Germany resisted a siege in Budapest, Hungary's capital, until February 1945. Vienna, Austria's capital, fell to Soviet soldiers in April. By then, Soviet troops occupied nearly all of eastern Europe.

With the Soviets and the rest of the Allied force pushing the Germans back, the Allies were close to winning the European front of World War II. Hitler's army was badly diminished after the Allies claimed key wins in France and eastern Europe. However, the Soviets' moves in eastern Europe would become consequential later as their ambitions for that region grew after the end of World War II.

Excited crowds filled Parliament Street in London, England, to celebrate Germany's surrender on May 7, 1945, ending World War II in Europe. The Allies declared May 8 as Victory in Europe Day, or V-E Day.

CHAPTER FIVE

Victory in Europe; Holocaust; consequences of World War II in Europe

The Allies began their final assault on Germany in early 1945. Soviet soldiers reached the Oder (*OH duhr*) River, about 40 miles (65 kilometers) east of Berlin, in January. Allied forces in the west occupied positions along the Rhine by early March.

British and Canadian forces cleared the Germans out of the Netherlands and swept into northern Germany. American and French forces raced toward the Elbe (*EHL buh*) River in central Germany. Hitler ordered his soldiers to fight to the death. But large numbers of German soldiers surrendered each day.

As they advanced, the Allies discovered horrifying evidence of Nazi brutality. Hitler had ordered the imprisonment and murder of millions of Jews and members of other minority groups in concentration camps. The starving survivors of the death camps gave proof of the terrible suffering of those who had already died. The full nature and reality of the Holocaust came to light in later months and years.

The Allies left the capture of Berlin to Soviet forces. By April 25, 1945, Soviet troops had surrounded the city. From a *bunker* (shelter) deep underground, Hitler ordered German soldiers to fight on. On April 30, however, Hitler killed himself rather than face defeat. With him died the Third Reich (Third Empire), the Nazi term for the empire in which they hoped to unite all Germanic peoples.

The fighting in Berlin claimed the lives of over 70,000 Soviet soldiers. The Germans propped up their remaining units with children and elderly reservists. Thousands of them died in that last week of fighting.

German Grand Admiral Karl Dönitz (DAY nihts) (1891-1980) briefly succeeded Hitler and arranged for Germany's surrender. On May 7, 1945, General Alfred Jodl (*AHL frayt YOHD uhl*) (1890-1946), chief of staff of the German armed forces, signed a statement of unconditional surrender at Eisenhower's headquarters in Reims (*reemz* or *rahnz*), France. World War II had ended in Europe. The Allies declared May 8 as Victory in Europe Day, or V-E Day.

The Holocaust

The Holocaust (*HOL uh kawst*) was the systematic, state-sponsored murder of Jews and others by the Nazis during World War II. Nazi dictator Adolf Hitler wanted to eliminate all Jews as part of his aim to conquer the world. By the end of the war, the Nazis had killed about 6 million Jewish men, women, and children—more than two-thirds of the Jews in Europe.

In addition to Jews, the Nazis systematically killed millions of other people whom Hitler regarded as racially inferior or politically dangerous. The largest groups included (1) Germans with physical handicaps or mental retardation, (2) Roma (sometimes called Gypsies), and (3) Slavs, particularly Poles and Soviet prisoners of war. Nazi victims also included many homosexuals, Jehovah's Witnesses, priests and ministers, members of labor unions, and Communists and other political opponents. Historians estimate that perhaps as many as 11 million people were killed, including the Jews. Many of the Holocaust victims were killed in specially constructed gas chambers, and their bodies were then

In 1894, Jewish French Army Captain Alfred Dreyfus was accused of selling military secrets to Germany. Dreyfus, shown here in 1898, was court-martialed and condemned to life imprisonment on Devils Island in French Guiana.

burned. The word *holocaust* means *a sacrificial offering that is completely burned.*

The Jews had faced persecution long before the Holocaust began. *Anti-Semitism* (prejudice against Jews) has existed since ancient times. Many early Christians mistrusted Jews because the Jews remained faithful to their own traditions and refused to convert to Christianity. In the mid-1500's, the German religious reformer Martin Luther issued ferocious attacks against the Jews for not adopting his new religion. He referred to the Jews as "venomous" and called for violence against them. In many cities, the Jews were forced to live in separate communities called *ghettos.* They had to pay special taxes, and they were not allowed to own land or enter certain occupations.

In the 1800's, many people began discriminating against Jews on racial rather than religious grounds. Many anti-Semitic writers insisted that Jews were an inferior race. Anti-Semitism became a powerful force in European politics. Many people considered the Jews responsible for society's troubles. In 1881, for example, when revolutionaries assassinated Czar Alexander II of Russia, the Jews were blamed. Many Russian Jews were then killed in organized massacres called *pogroms (poh GROMZ)*.

In 1894, Captain Alfred Dreyfus (*DRAY fuhs*), a French army officer and a Jew, was accused of selling military secrets. Although the case against Dreyfus was weak, a court-martial condemned him to life imprisonment. After the verdict was announced, his opponents chanted in the streets, "Death to Dreyfus! Death to the Jews!" In 1906, he was cleared of all charges.

Adolf Hitler, the leader of the Nazi Party, became head of the German government in 1933. He quickly moved to make himself a dictator. Germany's defeat in World War I (1914-1918) and a worldwide depression in the early 1930's had left the country's economy in ruins. Hitler blamed the Jews for Germany's problems, and he made anti-Semitism a government policy.

On April 1, 1933, Hitler's government sponsored a nationwide boycott of Jewish stores and other businesses. In the next several months, the government passed laws that barred Jews from specific occupations. Jews were excluded from civil service, for example, and from the fields of education and culture, and they could no longer farm the land.

The Nuremberg laws of 1935 stripped Jews of citizenship. Jews were forbidden to marry non-Jews. The laws set forth definitions of who was a Jew and who was a part-Jew, also known as a *Mischling* (*MIHSH lihng*) (mixed blood). For example, a person who had at least three Jewish

The Nazis forced Jews and others into concentration camps during the Holocaust, which took place during World War II. Most of the camps became centers for slave labor. Some, known as death camps, were centers for mass murder. This map shows a fraction of the hundreds of camps throughout Europe.

grandparents was classified as a Jew. Someone with one Jewish grand-parent might be classified as a Mischling.

In the next three years, the Nazi government continued to deprive Jews of their rights and possessions. Jews could not sit on park benches or swim in public pools. The government seized Jewish businesses as well as personal property. The discrimination was an effort to force Jews to emigrate so Germany would be *Judenrein* (*YOO dehn ryn*) (free of Jews). Thousands of Jews did leave the country, though they were per-mitted to take little with them. But many Jews were trapped because other countries would not accept them in large numbers.

Nazi persecution reached a new height on Nov. 9, 1938. Beginning that night and continuing for about 24 hours, Nazis destroyed thousands of Jewish-owned businesses and burned most synagogues in Germany and

The broken windows of a Jewish-owned printing business in Berlin show some of the damage done on *Kristallnacht* (Crystal Night), the night of Nov. 9-10, 1938. On that night, called the Night of Broken Glass in English, Nazis attacked Jews and destroyed Jewish businesses and synagogues throughout Germany and Austria.

Austria. They beat Jews in the streets and attacked them in their homes, killing dozens of Jews. They arrested about 30,000 Jews and sent them to *concentration camps* (camps for political prisoners). The night became known as *Kristallnacht* (*KRIHS tahl nahkt*), a German word meaning *Crystal Night*. In English, it is called the Night of Broken Glass.

After World War II began in 1939, Germany's powerful war machine conquered country after country in Europe. Millions more Jews came under German control. The Nazis killed many of them and sent others to concentration camps. Also, Nazis moved many Jews from towns and villages into city ghettos. They later sent these people, too, to concentration camps. Although many Jews thought the ghettos would last, the Nazis saw ghetto confinement as only a temporary measure. Sometime in early 1941, the Nazi leadership finalized the details of a policy decision labeled "the final solution of the Jewish question." This policy called for the murder of every Jew—man, woman, and child—under German rule.

The slaughter began with Germany's invasion of the Soviet Union in June 1941. Special squads of Hitler's SS Schutzstaffel (*SHOOTS shtah fuhl*) troops accompanied advancing German forces. (*Schutzstaffel* is German for *protection squadron*.) These killing squads, called *Einsatz-gruppen (YN sahtz GROO pehn)* (Mission Groups), rounded up Jews, Roma, and Soviet leaders, and shot them to death one by one. The face-to-face killing became difficult for the killers, and the Nazis soon sought a more impersonal and efficient method of *genocide (JEHN uh syd)* (extermination of an entire people). They began using sealed vans.

Nazi soldiers force Jews out of the Warsaw, Poland, ghetto and toward trains headed to death camps. Jews in the Warsaw ghetto revolted against the Nazis in April and May 1943. Although the Jews were poorly armed, it took about four weeks for the Nazis to end the uprising.

The prisoners choked to death on exhaust fumes as the van traveled to a burial pit.

At the Wannsee Conference, held in Berlin in January 1942, Nazi leaders further systematized the killing. They decided that Jews throughout German-occupied territory would be evacuated to concentration camps in eastern Europe. These camps would become centers for slave labor and mass murder.

The first Nazi concentration camps were organized in 1933, shortly after Hitler came to power. By the late 1930's, the facilities held tens of thousands of political prisoners arrested by the Nazis. In the early 1940's, several new camps were established, with specially constructed gas chambers disguised as showers.

For the Jews who had been confined in ghettos, the next step was what the Nazis called *deportation*. The Nazis herded the Jews into railroad freight cars to be taken to the camps.

When the Jews arrived at a camp, an SS physician singled out the young and able-bodied. The others were sent directly to the gas chambers. The guards seized the belongings of those who were to die. As many as 2,000 prisoners were sent into the gas chambers at one time. SS personnel poured containers of poison gas down an opening. Within 20 to 30 minutes, the new arrivals were dead. The guards shaved the heads of the corpses and removed any gold teeth from their mouths. Then they burned the bodies in crematoriums or open pits.

The able-bodied prisoners had their heads shaved and their belongings seized. Camp personnel tattooed a number on the arm of each person. From then on, the prisoners were identified by their number instead of by name. These prisoners were forced to work long hours under cruel conditions. When they were too weak to work any longer, they too were killed or left to die. There were six death camps, all in German-occupied

Jews arrive at Auschwitz concentration camp in May 1944. Auschwitz was the largest and most notorious of the six death camps run by the Nazis in German-occupied Poland during World War II. About 1 1/4 million people were murdered there.

Poland—Auschwitz (*OWSH vihts*), Bełzec (*BEHW zheht*), Chełmno (*HEHL muh noh*), Majdanek (*my DAH nehk*), Sobibór (*SOH bee bawr*), and Treblinka (*truh BLIHNG kuh*). Auschwitz was the largest and most notorious. It was a slave labor camp as well as a killing center. About 1 1/4 million people were murdered there.

Hundreds of other concentration camps operated in Germany and German-occupied territories during the war. None of these camps was established solely for killing, but the conditions in all of them were so harsh that hundreds of thousands of prisoners died of starvation and disease. In some camps, some inmates—many of them children—died after Nazi physicians performed cruel medical experiments on them.

In the last months of the war, the Allied forces, including American, British, and Soviet troops, swept through Europe. The Nazis hastened to empty some camps to remove witnesses to their cruelty. They crowded camp inmates into boxcars or forced the prisoners to walk to other camps behind the lines. The forced marches, made in winter with few provisions, claimed so many victims that they were known as *death marches.*

During the Holocaust, the Nazis kept their actions as secret as possible, and they deceived their victims in many ways to prevent resistance. Initially, the Jews in the ghettos either were unaware of the slaughter planned for them or simply could not believe it was happening. Some tried to pacify the Nazis, hoping they would be left in peace. Others tried sabotage or escape.

Armed resistance was not the first response of the Jews. They tried to thwart the Nazis by nonviolent means. Also, it was difficult and dangerous for the Jews to obtain weapons. Little help was available to them. Anti-Semitism was widespread, and Jewish resistance did not have popular support. Jewish fighters could not disappear among the population because non-Jews might betray them. Jewish leaders in the ghettos knew that the Nazis could kill everyone in the ghetto in revenge for the actions of a few resisters. But many Jews who managed to escape the ghettos joined secret bands of fighters against the Nazis. And some non-Jewish individuals risked their lives to smuggle Jews to safety.

Some Jews in ghettos, slave labor camps, and death camps did fight. In 1943, for example, thousands of Jews revolted in the Warsaw ghetto, in Poland. Although the Jews were surrounded and poorly armed, they held out for about four weeks. But the Nazis either killed or sent to death camps all of the 60,000 Jews in the ghetto.

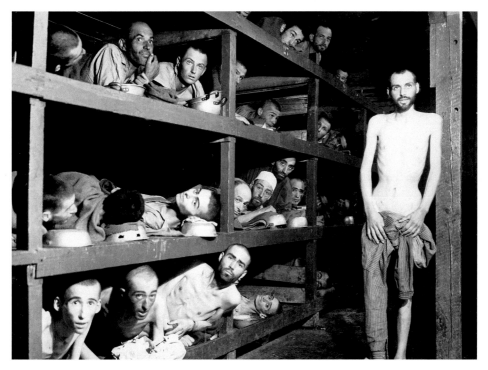

Survivors of the Nazi concentration camp Buchenwald—some too weak to stand—provided proof of Nazi savagery. This picture of inmates of Buchenwald was taken just a few days after United States troops liberated the camp. The Nazis imprisoned and murdered millions of Jews, Slavs, and members of other targeted groups.

In 1943, uprisings took place at the Treblinka and Sobibór death camps. In 1944, prisoners at Auschwitz revolted and set fire to a crematorium. A few prisoners escaped during each uprising, but most were killed. Such revolts were often acts of desperation. They erupted when the Jews understood Nazi intentions and had abandoned hope of survival. The fighters also hoped to protect Jewish honor and to avenge Jewish deaths.

As the Allies advanced through Europe in 1944 and 1945, they found millions of *displaced persons* living in countries not their own. Most of these people, including many Jews, eventually returned to their homelands. However, many of the Jews had nowhere to go. Their homes had been destroyed, and their families murdered. The presence of so many Jews on German soil, living among their former killers, pressured world leaders to find a place where the Jews could go. The Jews themselves wanted an independent Jewish state in Palestine, the ancient Jewish homeland in the Middle East.

In the late 1800's, members of a Jewish movement called Zionism had begun promoting immigration of Jews to Palestine. In the early 1900's, the British rulers of Palestine had pledged support for a national homeland there for the Jews. But the Arabs who lived in the area had opposed it, and severe fighting had broken out several times during the 1920's and 1930's. In 1939, the British had begun limiting Jewish immigration to Palestine to gain Arab support for the Allies in World War II. Both during and after the war, Palestine's Jews fought bitterly against the restrictions. The British submitted the problem to the United Nations (UN). In 1947, the UN proposed dividing Palestine into an Arab state and a Jewish one. In May 1948, the state of Israel officially came into existence and opened its borders to receive the Jews.

In the fall of 1943, Allied leaders declared their determination to bring the Nazi leaders to justice for their wartime behavior. The outrage of the Allies only intensified during the final months of the war when the killing centers were discovered. The Nuremberg trials took place from 1945 to 1949. They were held in Nuremberg, Germany, where the Nazi Party had staged huge rallies.

The Nazi leaders were charged with four major types of crimes—conspiracy to commit crimes against peace, crimes against peace, war crimes, and crimes against humanity. Conspiracy to commit crimes against peace included the planning of a war of aggression. Crimes

German Nazi SS officer Otto Ohlendorf stands (right, wearing headphones) at the witness stand during the Nazi war crimes trials in Nuremberg, Germany, in 1946. Ohlendor looks at a Nazi organizational chart.

against peace included carrying out such a war. War crimes included the murder of prisoners of war and of civilians, and the destruction of towns and cities. Crimes against humanity included deporting civilians and using them for slave labor as well as persecuting and murdering people for their political beliefs, race, or religion.

On Dec. 9, 1948, the United Nations passed the Genocide Convention, which was designed to overcome the claims of Nuremberg defendants that they had violated no law. The convention made genocide a crime. On Dec. 10, the UN adopted the Universal Declaration of Human Rights.

In the 1990's, Jewish groups pressured those who had profited from the Holocaust to compensate Holocaust victims or their descendants. Groups that paid reparations included the German government, certain Swiss banks, and some German companies.

The Secret War

Throughout World War II, a secret war was fought between the Allies and the Axis. The goals of the secret war were to obtain information about each other's activities and weaken each other's war effort. Codebreakers tried to figure out secret communications. Spies worked behind enemy lines to gather information. Saboteurs tried to disrupt activities on the home front. Many people in Axis-held territories joined undercover resistance groups that opposed the occupying forces. All the warring nations used propaganda to influence public opinion.

Soon after the outbreak of World War II, the United Kingdom obtained, with the help of Polish spies, an Enigma machine. Germany used Enigma machines to code secret messages. British mathematicians and codebreakers solved the machine's electronic coding procedures. The ability to read many of Germany's wartime communications was known as the *Ultra secret*. Ultra helped the Allies defeat Germany. During the 1940 Battle of Britain, Ultra supplied warning of where and when the Luftwaffe planned to attack. Ultra also helped Montgomery defeat the Germans in Egypt in 1942 by providing him with Rommel's battle plan.

The British carefully guarded the Ultra secret. They were cautious about using their knowledge so that Germany would not change its coding procedures. The Germans never discovered that the United Kingdom had broken their code.

The warring nations trained spies and saboteurs. Spies reported on

German forces depended on Enigma machines to encode and decode secret messages transmitted over the radio during World War II. The Enigma machine is on the left. (Photo courtesy of Helge Fykse, Norway)

troop movements, defense build-ups, and other developments behind enemy lines. Spies of Allied nations also supplied resistance groups with weapons and explosives. Saboteurs (*sab uh TURZ*) hampered the enemy's war effort by blowing up factories and bridges and organizing slowdowns in war plants.

Germany had spies in many countries. But its efforts at spying were less successful than those of the Allies. The U.S. government set up a wartime agency called the Office of Strategic Services (OSS) to engage in spying and sabotage. The OSS worked closely with a similar British agency, the Special Operations Executive. The Soviet Union operated

An Enigma decryption machine, called a "bombe," is shown above. This machine, made by National Cash Register of Dayton, Ohio, eliminated all possible encryptions from intercepted messages until it arrived at the correct solution.

networks of spies in Allied nations as well as in Germany and Japan.

Resistance groups sprang up in every Axis-occupied country. Resistance began with individual acts of defiance against the occupiers. Gradually, like-minded people banded together and worked in secret to oppose the Axis. Resistance groups expanded their activities as the war continued. The resistance published and distributed illegal newspapers. Resistance workers rescued Allied aircrews shot down behind enemy lines. The resistance also gathered information about the enemy and sabotaged military installations.

In such countries as France, Yugoslavia, and Burma, resistance groups organized bands of fighters. Resistance fighters staged raids, ambushes, and guerrilla attacks against the occupation forces. The French resistance interfered with German efforts to repel the Allied invasion of Normandy in 1944. Norwegian resistance workers destroyed a German-bound shipment of *heavy water,* a substance needed to make atomic weapons. Yugoslavia had the most effective resistance movement of all—the Partisans. With Allied help, the Partisans drove the Germans out of Yugoslavia in 1944.

In Germany, a small underground movement opposed the Nazis. In July 1944, a group of German army officers planted a bomb intended to kill Hitler. However, Hitler escaped the explosion with minor injuries. The plotters were arrested and executed.

Resistance workers caught by the Nazis faced certain death. German soldiers rounded up and executed hundreds of civilians as *reprisals* (punishment) for acts of rebellion against the Nazi occupiers.

All the warring nations used propaganda to win support for their policies. Governments aimed propaganda at their own people and at the enemy. Radio broadcasts reached the largest audiences. Motion pictures, posters, and cartoons were also used.

The Nazis were masters of propaganda. Joseph Goebbels (*YOH zehf GERH buhls*) (1897-1945) directed Germany's Ministry of Propaganda and Enlightenment. It controlled publications, radio programs, motion pictures, and the arts in Germany and German-occupied Europe. The ministry worked to convince people of the superiority of German culture and of Germany's right to rule the world. As the war turned in favor of the Allies, the Germans claimed to be saving the world from the evils of Communism.

Mussolini stirred the Italians with dreams of restoring Italy to the

Two propaganda versions of Adolf Hitler show the German dictator from opposite viewpoints. A pro-Hitler poster, left, portrays him as a heroic warrior crowned with a halo of light. An anti-Hitler cartoon, right, pictures him as a ridiculous, loudmouthed tyrant.

glory of ancient Rome. British Broadcasting Corporation (BBC) newscasts provided truthful information about the day's fighting to the European mainland. The Nazis made it a crime for people in Germany and German-held lands to listen to BBC broadcasts. The U.S. government established the Office of War Information to encourage American support for the war effort. In 1942, the Voice of America, a government radio service, began broadcasting to Axis-occupied countries.

The warring countries also engaged in psychological warfare. It was intended to destroy the enemy's will to fight. American planes dropped leaflets over Germany that told of Nazi defeats. The Axis nations employed English-speaking radio announcers to weaken the morale of

Allied soldiers. Mildred Gillars (1900-1988), an American known as "Axis Sally," made broadcasts for Germany.

Consequences of World War II in Europe

World War II took more lives and caused more destruction than any other war. Altogether, about 70 million people served in the armed forces of the Allied and Axis nations. About 20 million of them lost their lives. The Soviet Union lost at least 7 1/2 million soldiers and about 10 million civilians, much more than any other country. American deaths came to about 400,000. The United Kingdom lost a similar amount. Germany lost 3 1/4 million military personnel. About 2 million Japanese military personnel died. Poland suffered 600,000 military deaths and nearly 6 million civilian dead. Italy, Romania, and Yugoslavia all lost 300,000 soldiers or more. Austria, France, and Hungary each lost more than 200,000.

World War II uprooted millions of people. By the war's end, more than 12 million displaced persons remained in Europe. They included orphans, prisoners of war, and survivors of Nazi concentration and slave labor camps. They also included people who had fled invading armies and war-torn areas. Other people were displaced by changes in national borders. For example, many Germans were expelled from Poland, Czechoslovakia, and other lands in eastern Europe that the Nazis had taken.

To help displaced persons, the Allies established the United Nations Relief and Rehabilitation Administration (UNRRA). UNRRA began operating in 1944 in areas freed from Nazi occupation. The organization set up camps for displaced persons. It provided them with food, clothing, and medical supplies. By 1947, most people had been resettled. However, about a million people still remained in camps. Many had fled from countries in eastern Europe. They refused to return to homelands that had come under Communist rule.

New power struggles arose after World War II ended. The war had exhausted the leading prewar powers of Europe and Asia. Germany and Japan ended the war in defeat. The United Kingdom and France were weakened. The United States and the Soviet Union emerged as the world's leading powers. Their wartime alliance soon collapsed. The Soviet Union sought to spread Communism in Europe and Asia. A struggle developed between the Communist world, led by the Soviet Union, and the non-Communist world, led by the United States. That struggle became known as the Cold War.

The United States had fought the Axis to preserve democracy. After the war, Americans found it impossible to return to the policy of isolation their country had followed before the war. Americans realized that they needed strong allies. They helped the war-torn nations—friend and foe alike—recover.

World War II had united the Soviet people behind a great patriotic effort. The Soviet Union came out of the war stronger than before, despite the destruction it had suffered. Before the war ended, the Soviet Union had absorbed three nations along the Baltic Sea—Estonia, Latvia, and Lithuania. It had also taken parts of Poland, Romania, Finland, and Czechoslovakia by mid-1945. At the end of the war, Soviet troops occupied most of eastern Europe. In March 1946, Churchill warned that an "iron curtain" had descended across Europe. It divided eastern Europe from western Europe. Behind the Iron Curtain, the Soviet Union helped Communist governments take power in Bulgaria, Czechoslovakia, Hungary, Poland, and Romania.

By 1947, Communists threatened to take control of Greece. The Soviet Union was demanding military bases in Turkey. That year, United States

Under the Marshall Plan, the United States sent about
$13 billion in economic aid—food, machinery, and other
products—to help rebuild Europe after World War II.

President Harry Truman announced that the United States would
provide military and economic aid to any country threatened by
Communism. American aid helped Greece and Turkey resist Communist aggression.

In 1948, the United States set up the Marshall Plan to help war-torn
nations in Europe rebuild their economies. Under the plan, 18 nations
received about $13 billion in food, machinery, and other goods. The
Soviet Union forbade countries in eastern Europe to participate in

Marshall Plan

The Marshall Plan encouraged European nations to work together for economic recovery after World War II. In June 1947, the United States agreed to administer aid to Europe if the countries would meet to decide what they needed. The official name of the plan was the European Recovery Program. It is called the Marshall Plan because Secretary of State,

and former general, George C. Marshall first suggested it.

U.S. Secretary of State George Marshall (second from left) discusses the Marshall Plan with President Harry Truman (left) and others at the White House in 1948.

The Marshall Plan began in April 1948, when Congress established the Economic Cooperation Administration (ECA) to administer foreign aid. Seventeen nations formed the Organization for European Economic Cooperation (OEEC) to assist the ECA and develop cooperation among its members. The United States sent about $13 billion in food, machinery, and other products to Europe. Aid ended in 1952.

In 1961, the Organisation for Economic Co-operation and Development (OECD) succeeded the OEEC. Twenty nations, including the United States and Canada, formed the OECD to promote the economic growth of member nations and aid developing areas.

A parade was held in Athens in 1947, honoring the Marshall Plan's millionth ton of food for Greece after World War II. Aid to Europe through the Marshall Plan ended in 1952.

Leaders of the Big Three Allied nations—the United States, the United Kingdom, and the Soviet Union—met for the last time at the Potsdam Conference in Potsdam, Germany, in July 1945, to discuss arrangements for dividing up Germany following its defeat in World War II. Present at the opening of the meeting were Soviet Premier Joseph Stalin (at the right of the table, holding a cigarette), U.S. President Harry S. Truman (left foreground, hands on table), and British Prime Minister Winston Churchill (at the upper left of the table, holding papers).

the Marshall Plan.

The nuclear age opened with the development of the atomic bomb during World War II. Many people believed that weapons of mass destruction would make war unthinkable in the future. They hoped that the world would learn to live in peace. But a race to develop ever more powerful weapons soon began.

At the end of World War II, only the United States knew how to build an atomic weapon. In 1946, the United States proposed the creation of an international agency that would control atomic energy and ban the

production of nuclear weapons. But the Soviet Union objected to an inspection system. The proposal was dropped. Soviet scientists developed an atomic bomb in 1949.

Before World War II ended, the Allies had decided on a military occupation of Germany after its defeat. They divided Germany into four zones. The United States, the Soviet Union, the United Kingdom, and France each occupied a zone. The four powers jointly administered the capital city of Berlin.

At the Potsdam Conference in July 1945, the Allies produced their

European occupation policy while the war with Japan continued. They agreed to abolish Germany's armed forces and to outlaw the Nazi Party. Germany lost territory east of the Oder and Neisse (*NY suh*) rivers. Most of the region went to Poland. The Soviet Union gained a corner of this territory.

The Allies brought to trial Nazi leaders accused of war crimes. The trials exposed the evils inflicted by Nazi Germany. Many leading Nazis were sentenced to death. The most important war trials took place in the German city of Nuremberg from 1945 to 1949.

Soon after the occupation began, the Soviet Union stopped cooperat-

In 1990, East and West Germany were reunited as a non-Communist country. The Reichstag is flying the German flag, a symbol of the reunification of the two countries.

ing with its Western Allies. It blocked all efforts to reunite Germany. The Western Allies gradually joined their zones into one economic unit. But the Soviet Union forbade its zone to join.

The city of Berlin lay deep within the Soviet zone of Germany. In June 1948, the Soviet Union sought to drive the Western powers from Berlin by blocking all rail, water, and highway routes to the city. For over a year, the Western Allies flew in food, fuel, and other goods to Berlin. The Soviet Union finally lifted the Berlin blockade in May 1949.

The Western Allies set up political parties in their zones and held elections. In September 1949, the three Western zones combined as the Federal Republic of Germany, also known as West Germany. In May 1955, the Western Allies signed a treaty ending the occupation of West Germany. They granted the country full independence. However, the treaty was not a general peace treaty because the Soviet Union refused to sign it. The Soviet Union set up a Communist government in its zone. In October 1949, the Soviet zone became the German Democratic Republic, also called East Germany.

In September 1990, the Soviet Union and the Western Allies signed a treaty to give up all their occupation rights in East and West Germany. In October 1990, Germany was reunited as a non-Communist nation.

Soon after World War II ended, the Allies began to draw up peace treaties with Italy and the other countries that fought against the Allies. The treaties limited the armed forces of the defeated countries. The agreements required the defeated countries to pay war damages. The treaties also called for territorial changes. Bulgaria gave up territory to Greece and Yugoslavia. Czechoslovakia gained land from Hungary. Italy gave up land to France, Yugoslavia, and Greece. Italy also lost its empire in Africa. Romania gained territory from Hungary, but in turn lost land to Bulgaria and the Soviet Union.

FIND OUT MORE!

Childers, Thomas. *The Third Reich: A History of Nazi Germany.* Simon & Schuster, 2017.

Holland, James. *The Rise of Germany, 1939-1941.* Atlantic Monthly Pr., 2015. *The Allies Strike Back, 1941-1943.* 2017.

Tucker, Spencer C. *World War II: The Definitive Encyclopedia and Document Collection.* 5 vols. ABC-Clio, 2016.

ACKNOWLEDGMENTS

Cover: © The Print Collector/ Getty Images; Imperial War Museum; © Yousuf Karsh, Library and Archives Canada; © Everett Historical/ Shutterstock; © FPG/ Hulton Archive/Getty Images
4-7 © Everett Historical/ Shutterstock
8 Public Domain
11 National Archives
12 National Library of Norway
15 © Roman Nerud, Shutterstock
16-17 © Everett Historical/ Shutterstock; © Ann Ronan Pictures/Print Collector/Getty Images
19 © Everett Historical/ Shutterstock
20-21 © Keystone/Getty Images; GureGipuzkoa/Kutxa Photograph Library (licensed under CC BY-SA 3.0)
22-23 Library of Congress; Public Domain
24-25 © Everett Historical/ Shutterstock; © Sovfoto/ UIG/Getty Images
27 Deutsches Bundesarchiv (licensed under CC-BY-SA 3.0)
28 Public Domain
31 © Everett Historical/ Shutterstock
33 © ullstein bild/Getty Images
35 Public Domain (Imperial War Museums)

37 © Art Media/Print Collector/Getty Images
38 © Everett Historical/ Shutterstock
41 WORLD BOOK map
43 Imperial War Museum
45 © Hans Wild, The LIFE Picture Collection/Getty Images
46 Imperial War Museum
48 © Margaret Bourke-White, The LIFE Picture Collection/Getty Images
51 © Everett Historical/ Shutterstock
52 Public Domain
55-58 © Everett Historical/ Shutterstock
56 WORLD BOOK map
59 WORLD BOOK map
60 © Bettmann/Getty Images
63 Library of Congress
65-67 Franklin D. Roosevelt Library
69 National Archives
70 Library of Congress
72 Imperial War Museum
73 WORLD BOOK map
74 © Everett Historical/ Shutterstock
75 WORLD BOOK map
76 Vsevolod Tarasevich, RIA Novosti archive (licensed under CC-BY-SA 3.0)
77 WORLD BOOK map
79 U.S. Air Force
80 National Archives
83-87 WORLD BOOK illustrations by Tony Gibbons
88 Library of Congress

90-91 Library of Congress; © PhotoQuest/Getty Images
92-93 U. S. Coast Guard
94-95 Russian International News Agency (licensed under CC-BY-SA 3.0)
96-97 August Ahrens, Deutsches Bundesarchiv (licensed under CC-BY-SA 3.0); © Alexander Ustinov, Slava Katamidze Collection/Getty Images
98 © Popperfoto/Getty Images
101 Public Domain
103 WORLD BOOK map
104-105 © Everett Historical/ Shutterstock; National Archives
107 Public Domain
109 National Archives
111 U.S. Army
113-114 U.S. Air Force
116 U.S. Army Center of Military History; National Archives, Collection U.S. Office of War Information
119 National Archives
120-121 National Archives; NASA; © Everett Historical/ Shutterstock
122-123 National Archives
124 © Bernard Bisson, Sygma/ Getty Images